INDIANA JONES

and the

TEMPLE OF DOOM ™

THE ILLUSTRATED SCREENPLAY

The Complete Script by
Willard Huyck & Gloria Katz

Introduction by
Steven Spielberg

Ballantine Books • New York

**Cover and interior designed by
Michaelis/Carpelis Design Associates, Inc.**

Frontispiece art by Bruce Wolfe
Art Direction by Christopher Werner

Library of Congress Catalog Card Number: 84-90819

ISBN 0-345-31879-X (hd cvr)
      0-345-31878 (pbk)

Manufactured in the United States of America

First Edition: November 1984

10 9 8 7 6 5 4 3 2 1

INTRODUCTION

Just how does one make a follow-up film to an exotic adventure like *Raiders of the Lost Ark*? That was the question all of us were asking in 1982 when it came time to put the second Indiana Jones serial onto the assembly line.

George Lucas, Indy's creator, teased me for weeks with previews about possible settings, subject matter, and fun-fantasy, but it wasn't until we hired writers Gloria Katz and Willard Huyck to do the screenplay that George told us, during a three-day story retreat, what we were going to be doing for the next two years.

George had a devilish grin on his face when he announced we would not be using the "Raiders" title, but instead would be calling it *Indiana Jones and the Temple of Death*.

We later prevailed upon George to change "Death" to "Doom," a word more in keeping with the spirit of the old Saturday matinee serials, to which we owe so much of our inspiration.

George and I didn't want to simply remake *Raiders of the Lost Ark*. We had already made that a fun-filled movie—and it carried with it a life of its own. Instead, George had in mind something much scarier—with black magic, human sacrifice, voodoo dolls, evil sorcerers, and subterranean villainy. This was going to be Dr. Jones' most frightening adventure.

All of us leapt at the chance to change milieu. And on June 7, 1982, the screenplay got under way.

One of our first notions was to begin the adventure in Shanghai, 1935. George wanted Indy to wear a tux in *Raiders of the Lost Ark*, but I objected to that side of Jones' occasionally mercenary character. But in his portrayal, Harrison Ford gave Indy so much battered class that the tux idea didn't seem so farfetched in our follow-up adventure. So when George suggested we start the movie with a musical number and Indy in dinner jacket, it seemed a real classy departure from what the audience had been conditioned to expect.

I offered the suggestion that Indy have a sidekick this time, an eleven-year-old Artful Dodger, a street orphan with a N.Y. Yankees cap and a lot of survival savvy. Bill and Gloria named him Short Round, after their dog, and when George suggested that Indy's love interest be a spoiled American torchsinger, the moll of a Shanghai ganglord, I suggested naming her after my dog, Willie.

After all, Indiana is named after George's dog, and all things being equal, this was the first of many in-gags that helped make *Temple of Doom* such a pleasure to work on.

This is pretty much how certain ideas in the screenplay were born; four people having a fine old time entertaining themselves, and hopefully the movie-going public.

Four months later the Huycks turned in their screenplay, an action-packed 130 pages of relentless thrills, chills and spills. Once I started to devour it, I couldn't put it down.

The production commenced shooting on April 18, 1983, and finished on September 8, 1983.

Douglas Slocombe photographed *Temple of Doom*, and it is one of his visual triumphs. Anthony Powell created the elaborate and sumptuous costumes, and I feel very fortunate to have worked with him. Elliot Scott, the dean of British Production Designers, produced some of the most imaginative sets I've ever had the privilege of working on.

George Gibbs, the enormously creative special floor effects expert, worked ingeniously and safely in the demolition of the rope bridge, the lava pit effects, and other wonders contained in the chamber of horrors that comprised the sinister second act of *Temple of Doom*.

I am indebted to the skills of crack editor Michael Kahn, Producer Robert Watts, Executive Producers Frank Marshall and George Lucas, and Associate Producer Kathleen Kennedy. The creative wizards at Industrial Light and Magic once again made the visually impossible miraculously credible.

I want to thank everyone for their dedication to this project, especially Harrison Ford, who continues to make the kind of contribution one only expects of a partner and collaborator, and newcomer Kate Capshaw, who is not as shrill in real life as I encouraged her to be as Willie Scott. And last, but not least, Ke Huy Quan—just about the most gifted newcomer to the movies I have ever worked with.

All these people and hundreds more helped to shape Indiana Jones into the popular entertainment it has now become.

Thank you all.

Steven Spielberg

FADE IN:

INTERIOR: THE CLUB OBI WAN—NIGHT

A Chinese GONG SOUNDS and patrons in the smoky nightclub quiet down and turn toward a giant papier-mâché dragon's head that dominates the stage. (Begin main titles.)

Now, the dragon's eyes light up, its enormous jaws exhale smoke, and out of the dragon's mouth walks the star of the stage show:

Above: storyboards by Edward Verreaux
Background: Production still by Keith Hamshere
Insets: Production stills by Keith Hamshere
Inset, lower right: Production still by Eva Sereny

WILLIE SCOTT, a dreamy beauty singing the Mandarin version of "Anything Goes." The orchestra wails the accompaniment, and a line of lovely showgirls, a mix of races, dances in the background. As the song ends and the soloist exits through the dragon's mouth, more dancers descend a giant stairway for a tap-dancing extravaganza as main titles end with:

SHANGHAI, 1935

A man in a tuxedo enters down the stairway and looks toward a table of three somber Chinese men. As he moves forward, a waiter, WU HAN, passes by him.

WU HAN: Be careful.

The man is INDIANA JONES. Elegant in a tuxedo—dressed to kill. He moves to the table with the Chinese men in suits and sits down. They stare coldly at Indiana.

INDIANA: Wah hung how, nee nah? Wah hwey ung jing chee jah loo nee kao soo wah shu shu.

LAO CHE looks angry and his men's smiles fade.

LAO: You never told me you spoke my language, Dr. Jones.
INDIANA: Only on special occasions.

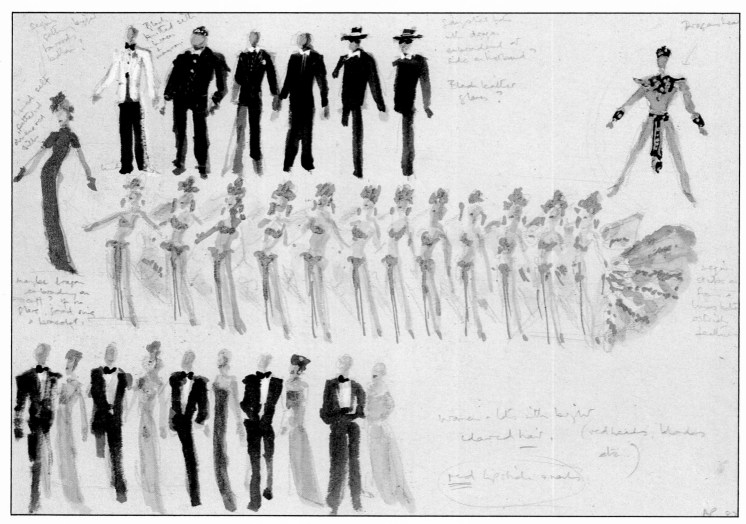

Lao Che, notorious crime-lord, is fifty, wealthy enough now to display some fat, but still muscular from his fight to the top of the garbabe heap. Sitting to Lao's right and left are his grim-looking sons CHEN and KAO KAN. Two more of Lao's men frisk Indy surreptitiously as they place a napkin in his lap.

LAO: So, it is true, you found the Nurhachi.
INDIANA: You know I did. Last night one of your boys…

Indiana looks across the table at Lao's son Chen, who resembles a bulldog and snarls like one now.

INDIANA *(continuing):* …tried to get Nurhachi without paying for him.

Indy stares pointedly at Chen, who lifts a recently bandaged hand from his lap.

LAO: You have insulted my son.
INDIANA: No, you have insulted me. I spared his life.

Kao Kan rises, voicing a Chinese protest, but his father motions him to sit down.

Now a pretty hand slips onto Lao's shoulder, and he looks up to see Willie Scott behind him. Willie is unaware of the explosive mood at the table and she smiles flirtatiously at Indiana.

WILLIE *(to Lao):* Aren't you going to introduce us?
LAO: This is Willie Scott. *(watching Indy)* This is Indiana Jones, the famous archaeologist.

Willie sits down between Lao and Indy. She starts to remove her gloves and coyly teases Indiana.

Opposite page: Costume sketches by Anthony Powell

Above: Photo by Eva Sereny Costume sketches by Anthony Powell

5

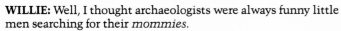

WILLIE: Well, I thought archaeologists were always funny little men searching for their *mommies.*
INDIANA *(correcting her):* Mummies.
LAO: Dr. Jones found Nurhachi for me. And he's going to deliver him…now.

Lao nods across the table and Indy sees Kao Kan aiming a pistol at him. Kao Kan cocks the gun.

WILLIE: Say, who is this Nurhachi?

As she speaks, Indy takes a carving fork from a tray and pulls Willie to him. She looks terrified at the fork Indy is poking against her ribs.

INDIANA *(to Kao Kan):* Put the gun away, sonny.

Kao Kan glances at his father. Lao finally nods to his son and he slips the pistol back into his pocket.

INDIANA *(to Lao):* Now, I suggest you give me what you owe me. Or anything goes.

6

The ritzy patrons at the tables nearby are unaware of the tawdry drama quietly unfolding at this table.

Willie eyes the fork and whimpers. She looks imploringly at Lao. Chen reaches into his pocket and sets a small pouch on the table's revolving center, spinning it over to Indy.

INDIANA *(to Willie):* Open it.

She pours ten gold coins from the pouch and places them on the table.

INDIANA: The diamond, Lao. The deal was for the diamond.

Willie spins the table and the coins stop in front of Lao. He reaches slowly into a pocket and brings out a small package, puts it on the table next to a glass of champagne and spins it back.

Willie unwraps the package and holds up an enormous diamond, turning it to catch the light.

WILLIE *(awestruck):* Oh, Lao.

She yelps as Indiana jabs the fork into her side, then reluctantly drops the diamond into his hand. Indy smiles and lifts his champagne glass in a toast.

INDIANA *(to Lao):* To your very good health.

Lao watches expectantly as Indiana moves the glass toward his lips.

Suddenly Willie stands angrily, jostling Indy's arm so that he spills some of his champagne.

WILLIE: Lao, he put a hole…he put *two* holes in my dress from Paris!

Lao sees Indy holding his champagne glass, not drinking, and he snarls at Willie—

LAO: Sit down!

Willie quickly obeys, sliding her chair out of Indiana's reach.

LAO *(to Indy):* Now, you bring me Nurhachi.
INDIANA: My pleasure.
WILLIE *(bewildered):* Who on earth is this Nurhachi?

Indiana motions to the waiter Wu Han to come closer to the table. He takes a carved jade urn from the tray and spins the urn across to Lao Che.

INDIANA: Here he is.
WILLIE *(to Lao):* This Nurhachi's a real small guy.
LAO: Inside are the remains of Nurhachi, the first Emperor of Manchu Dynasty.

Indiana drinks from his champagne glass, as Lao and his sons watch in sudden interest.

INDIANA *(toasting Nurhachi):* Welcome home, old boy.

Indiana drains his glass and sets it on the table, as Lao, Chen, and Kao Kan begin to chuckle in delight.

LAO: And now, you give me the diamond.
INDIANA: Are you trying to develop a sense of humor, or am I going deaf?

The three Chinese now laugh openly, as Lao, laughing, holds a small glass vial up to view.

WILLIE: What's that?
LAO: Antidote.
INDIANA: To what?
LAO: The poison you just drank, Dr. Jones.

Chen and Kao Kan burst out laughing again, as Indiana rubs a finger on the inside of his champagne glass, finding residue at the bottom of it. He swallows and feels sick, wondering if it's fear or the poison already taking effect. Indiana is sweating. Willie looks at him and sees Indy's hand shaking.

LAO *(continuing):* The poison works fast, Dr. Jones.

Willie gasps, then yells as Indiana pulls her in front of him and jabs a fork against her side. The waiter Wu Han, still holding his tray, moves to stand behind Indy.

WILLIE *(scared):* Lao!
INDIANA *(threatening):* Lao.
LAO *(laughs):* You keep the girl. I'll find another.

Opposite page: Costume sketches by Anthony Powell; Production still by Keith Hamshere

Above: Storyboards by Edward Verreaux Director Steven Spielberg; Photo by Keith Hamshere

Chen and Kao Kan stop laughing and tense as Indiana signals to Wu Han. The waiter, who is standing behind Indy, raises his tray to reveal a pistol aimed at the crime-lord.

INDIANA *(smiling at Wu Han):* Good service here.
WILLIE *(puzzled):* That's not a waiter.
INDIANA: Wu Han's an old friend. *(to Lao)* Game's not over, Lao. Antidote.

At a table behind them, a man pops a champagne cork and his female guests laugh merrily. There is the sound of another cork popping. And another. Wu Han looks puzzled and picks up a broken champagne glass on his tray. A red stain appears on his shirt and he begins to sag. Across the table, Kao Kan holds a smoking pistol with a silencer, now pointing at Indiana.

WU HAN: Indy!

Indy stands and grabs Wu Han, easing the phony waiter into the chair he just vacated. The muffled shooting hasn't attracted any attention. The nightclub activity continues as Indy speaks emotionally to his dying friend.

INDIANA: Don't worry, Wu Han, I'll get you outta here.

In pain, Wu Han looks at Indy and struggles to speak.

WU HAN: Not this time, Indy. *(smiling bravely)* I've followed you on many adventures, but into the great Unknown Mystery, I go first, Indy.

Wu Han dies and slumps forward. Indiana is shattered by the death of his old friend.

LAO: Don't be sad, Dr. Jones. You will soon be joining him.

Indy's gaze shifts from his dead friend to Lao's sneering face. Then Indy sees the murderous Chen giggling perversely. Indy's anger is compounded by the poison burning in his gut, and his vision of Chen's ugly face blurs.

CHEN *(laughing):* Too much to drink, Dr. Jones?

Indy stands up unsteadily. Kao Kan, holding the gun, assumes he's about to keel over from the poison—but Indy staggers backwards, colliding with a real waiter and the cart of roast pigeons that he's just set afire.

Indy grabs the skewer of pigeons flambé and hurls it across the table! Kao fires and misses—and screams as the skewer stabs into his chest and the burning pigeons flame in front of his horrified face!

This the other tables definitely notice. There are screams and all hell breaks loose. Indiana dives past Willie, knocking the precious diamond out of her hand. As he crashes onto the table, he misses the vial and knocks it to the floor.

As Indiana and Lao exchange threats in Chinese, Indy lands a punch on Chen, knocking him backwards, and as the melee builds, both the vial of antidote and the diamond Willie is holding go spinning across the floor.

Indiana scrambles after the rolling vial. People keep kicking it, shoving and hitting him as he reels around the room. Two men lift him on a serving cart and push. As he rolls by he reaches for the antidote but misses again! Willie spots the diamond. She smiles and reaches to get it just as an elegantly shod woman's foot kicks it away. Willie pounds on the floor in frustration.

Opposite page: Costume sketches by Anthony Powell; Production still by Keith Hamshere

Above: Storyboards by Edward Verreaux Production still by Keith Hamshere

*Above: Storyboards by
Edward Verreaux
Above, right: Production still by
Eva Sereny
Production still by
Keith Hamshere*

WILLIE: Nuts!

Near the bandstand, Indiana spots the vial across the floor and dives for it, sliding. Willie crawls toward the diamond from the other side. Both vial and diamond are kicked again as they crawl through and around people's legs.

INDIANA: The antidote?
WILLIE: Where's the diamond?

The music changes and the showgirls dance forward from the stage beginning the next show. Lao's hoods run in and Lao shouts orders at them in Chinese. They begin throwing axes at Indy, trapping him against a statue near the stage.

Willie spots the diamond, just as toppling ice buckets send a shower of ice across the floor—totally camouflaging the diamond.

WILLIE *(shrieks):* No!

She finds the vial of antidote and holds it up, as dozens of balloons start to fall from overhead. Indiana sees her.

INDIANA *(shouts):* Stay there!

Willie slips the vial inside the bodice of her gown, and Indy fights his way towards her, struggling through the drifting balloons and fighting off Lao's hoods. He weaves back and forth, then throws a glass of champagne into his face to clear his head.

Chen opens fire with a machine gun as Indy takes cover behind the giant silver gong. Bullets flying around him, Indiana runs across the stage and grabs a broadsword from the Chinese warrior statue. Indiana swings the sword toward the enormous gong and cuts the cord holding it in place.

The giant gong rolls and echoes as it crashes down. Indiana ducks behind it as it gains momentum and rolls across the dance floor.

Using the gong as an enormous shield, Indiana evades the gunfire exploding. Bullets ricochet off the rolling silver gong as he runs behind it.

Ahead, Willie hurries toward an exit. She hears something and turns—her eyes go wide as she sees the mammoth gong bearing down on her!

Willie yells as Indiana grabs her arm and pulls her behind the gong with him.

INDIANA: Come on!
WILLIE: I don't wanna go!

As bullets clang against the gong, Indiana and Willie run behind it. Willie hollers as they head directly for a towering, floor-to-ceiling window!

Indiana grabs Willie around the waist and, after the huge gong crashes through the stained-glass window, they both fly after it!

EXTERIOR: THE CLUB OBI WAN—NIGHT

In a shower of sparkling glass, the enormous gong sails out and crashes down a sloping, tiled roof. Indiana Jones and Willie Scott hurtle into the night air after it!

The gong rolls down the roof and they hit the tiles behind it, Indiana holding onto Willie as they roll one over the other toward the edge. Willie screams as they fall into thin air!

Their entwined bodies plummet three stories: ripping through one awning, rolling off the next, until they cling, feet dangling, above the street.

WILLIE (to Indiana): Who *are* you?

A Duesenberg rolls up and squeals to a stop beneath them. Indy lets go and drops through the convertible top. Willie follows.

INTERIOR: THE DUESENBERG

Willie is wide-eyed, speechless, and amazed to be alive. In the driver's seat is an eleven-year-old Chinese urchin, SHORT ROUND, wearing a New York Yankees baseball cap.

SHORT ROUND: Wow! Holy smoke! Crash landing!
INDIANA: Short Round, step on it!
SHORT ROUND: Okey dokey, Dr. Jones. Hold onto your potatoes!
WILLIE: For cryin' out loud, there's a *kid* driving the car!

The Chinese kid turns his baseball cap bill-backwards and steps on the gas with a block of wood tied to the bottom of his foot. The tires squeal as the car roars off. Willie and Indy are thrown against the seat.

WILLIE: Oh!

Storyboards by Edward Verreaux

EXTERIOR: THE NIGHTCLUB—NIGHT

The Duesenberg races past the entrance to the nightclub as Lao and his men rush out and jump into a black sedan. The sedan screeches off in pursuit of the Duesenberg.

EXTERIOR: SHANGHAI STREET—NIGHT

The Duesenberg tears through the narrow streets, scattering pedestrians and knocking down strings of lanterns spanning the streets. Bullets explode as amazed sailors and prostitutes watch the cars zoom past.

A lantern shatters on the hood of the car.

INTERIOR: THE DUESENBERG—NIGHT

SHORT ROUND: Wow!
INDIANA *(to Willie):* Where's the antidote?

In the back seat, Indiana is intent on his most immediate need. He grabs Willie and reaches into the bodice of her dress.

WILLIE: Listen, I just met you, for Christ sake.
INDIANA: Let me have it.
WILLIE: Oh, I'm not that kind of girl.

Short Round looks disapprovingly over his shoulder as Indy continues to search inside Willie's dress. Indiana withdraws his hand, having finally found the vial. He opens it quickly, tips the vial to his lips, and grimaces as he swallows the stuff.

SHORT ROUND: Hey, Dr. Jones. No time for love. We've got company.
WILLIE: Ohh, I hope you choke!

Gunfire suddenly explodes, bullets whizz through the canvas top, and the rear window shatters and sprays glass! Willie ducks and cringes terrified in the corner.

WILLIE: No shooting!

Indy pokes his gun through the broken window and starts firing back at their pursuers. Then he turns and looks ahead.

EXTERIOR: THE STREET—NIGHT

In the narrow street, the Duesenberg is trapped directly behind a rickshaw carrying a sailor and his girl. Short Round exchanges some angry words with the protesting rickshaw driver, who is unable or unwilling to pull aside.

INTERIOR: THE DUESENBERG—NIGHT

SHORT ROUND: Okay, you asked for it!

His foot with the block of wood attached hits the accelerator, and the hood of the car lifts the rickshaw into the air, the wailing driver dangling from the poles in front. Short Round hits the brake and the rickshaw sails off, crashing into a vendor's tent.

SHORT ROUND: This is fun!

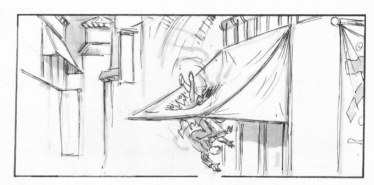

All storyboards by
Edward Verreaux
Production still by Jeff Marks

SHORT ROUNDS POPS UP IN F.G. "WOW! HOLY SMOKE... CRASH LANDING!"

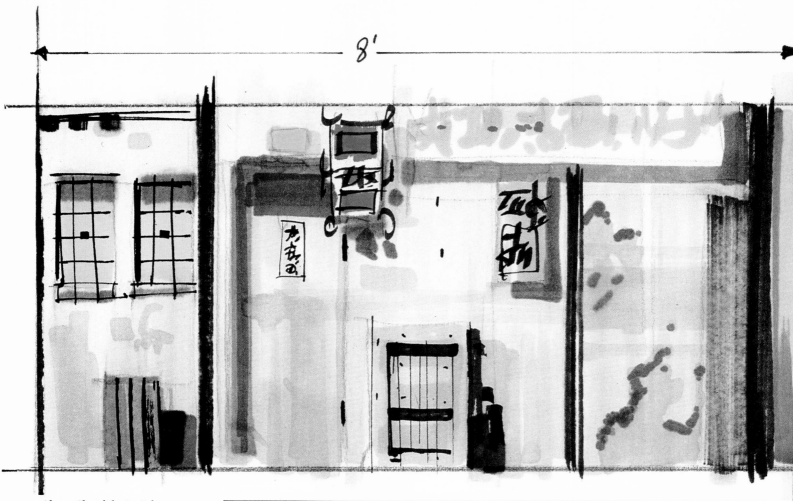

*Above: Sketch by Joe Johnston
Production stills by Ralph Nelson, Jr.*

*Opposite page: Storyboards by
Edward Verreaux*

Sketches by Joe Johnston

Short Round continues his lunatic drive. In the back seat, Indiana turns to Willie.

INDIANA: Here, hold this.

He hands her his revolver, and she gasps, juggling the hot metal from one hand to the other. The gun drops from her hand out the window and bounces on the running board as Indiana turns back to her.

INDIANA: Where's my gun? *(shouts)* Where's my gun?
WILLIE: I burnt my fingers, and I *cracked* a nail!

EXTERIOR: NANG TAO AIRFIELD—NIGHT

The Duesenberg swings around a curve and skids through gravel toward the airfield. Short Round wheels the car past the small terminal to the cargo area.

A trimotor is revving its engines as the Duesenberg squeals to a stop and Indy jumps out with Willie. Short Round grabs a small bag out of the car and runs after them.

At the boarding gate WEBER, an officious, prissy English airline official, runs to meet them.

WEBER: Ah, Dr. Jones, I'm, ah, Weber. I spoke with your *(eyeing Shorty curiously)* assistant. Ah, we've managed to secure three seats. But there might be a slight inconvenience as you will be riding on a cargo full of live poultry.
WILLIE: Is he kidding?!
WEBER *(icily):* Madame, it was the best I could do at such short notice. *(smiling suddenly)* Heavens—aren't you Willie Scott, the famous American female vocalist?

*Top: Sketch by Joe Johnston
Production stills by Ralph Nelson, Jr.*

Production stills by Ralph Nelson, Jr.
Sketch by Joe Johnston

Weber and Willie walk toward the revving trimotor, chatting away. At the plane, Indiana and Weber shake hands.

INDIANA (to Weber): Owe ya a gin.

Meanwhile, Lao's sedan stops outside the loading area and he and Chen stand watching at the gate. Indiana stands in the plane's door and throws a triumphant mock salute at the crime lord.

INDIANA (laughs): Nice try, Lao Che.

He pulls the door closed behind him and we see the legend painted on the door.

LAO CHE AIR FREIGHT

At the fence, Lao Che and Chen laugh gleefully as the plane turns and begins to taxi toward the runway. As the cockpit turns toward them, the copilot waves conspiratorially to Lao Che.

LAO CHE (laughs): Good-bye, Dr. Jones.

The plane lifts off the runway silhouetted against the clouds and the first light of dawn.

INTERIOR: THE PLANE

A door opens at the rear of the plane and Indiana Jones enters, wearing more familiar attire: a beat-up leather jacket over a khaki shirt and a snap-brim hat. He weaves through the cargo cases full of live poultry, carrying his rolled-up tuxedo.

Up front, Willie brushes feathers off as she tries to fix her hair. Willie puts on Indy's dinner jacket and watches him hook his coiled bullwhip over a crate.

WILLIE: So, what're you supposed to be, a lion tamer?

INDIANA: I'm allowing you to tag along, so why don't you give your mouth a rest? Okay, doll?

WILLIE *(indignantly):* What do you mean, "tag along"? Ever since you got into my club, you haven't been able to take your eyes off me.

INDIANA: Oh, yeah?

He leans back and tips his hat down *over his eyes to go to sleep.*

DISSOLVE TO:

EXTERIOR: THE PLANE

Above: Costume sketch by Anthony Powell
Sketch by Joe Johnston

Director Steven Spielberg; Photo by
Ralph Nelson, Jr.
Production still by Ralph Nelson, Jr.
Sketch by Joe Johnston

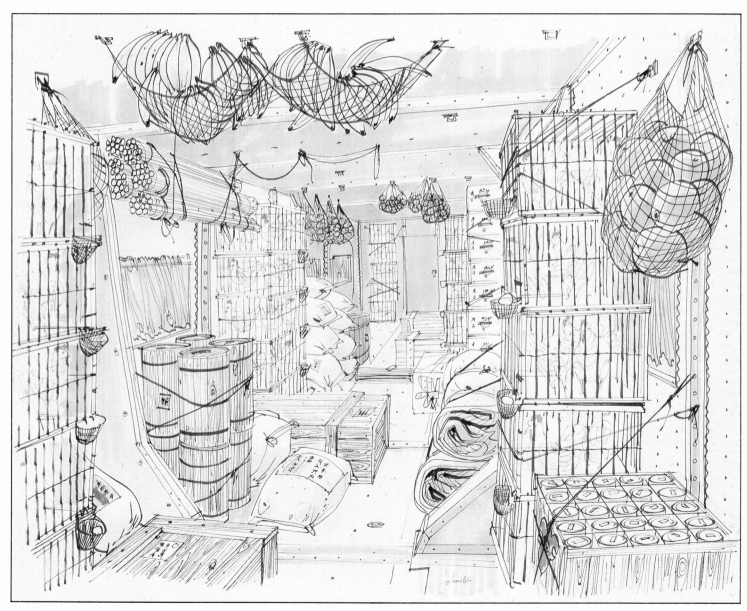

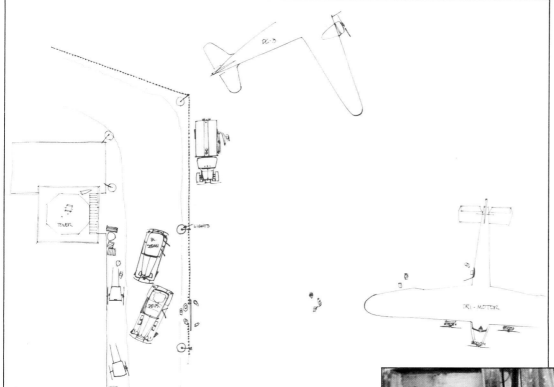

Sketch by Joe Johnston
Production stills by Ralph Nelson, Jr.

MAP over airplane showing its flight to Shanghai…to Chungking …moving west…

DISSOLVE TO:

INTERIOR: THE COCKPIT—LATER

The curtain between cockpit and cabin opens cautiously and the copilot peers out. Inside the passenger cabin Willie sleeps, wearing Indiana's tuxedo. Shorty has his head against Indy's side, both of them sound asleep.

The pilot and copilot consult in Chinese, and then the pilot pulls the fuel dump switch.

EXTERIOR: THE PLANE

Gasoline spews out of the plane's fuel tanks.

INTERIOR: THE CARGO AREA

The pilot laughs as he and the copilot, parachutes strapped to their backs, step over the sleeping passengers to the rear door. The draft from the open door makes feathers fly and the squawking chickens awaken Willie as the pilot bids them good-bye and jumps after his copilot.

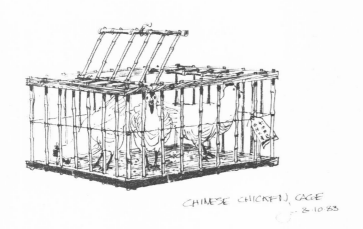

CHINESE CHICKEN CAGE
8.10.83

```
EXT. WALL OF CHINA - DAY
HIGH ANGLE. Tri-motor flys above the wall
of China.
```

NOTES:

Willie gets up and goes to the cockpit, looks inside and sees the empty pilots' chairs...and a range of snow-covered mountains through the windscreen.

WILLIE: Oh, no. Oh, no.

She races back to the cargo hold and begins shaking Indiana frantically.

WILLIE: Mister. Oh, Mister, wake up! Mister!
SHORT ROUND: You call him Dr. Jones, doll!
WILLIE: Okay. Dr. Jones. Dr. Jones! Wake up, please!

INDIANA: Hmmm. Are we there already? Oh, good.
WILLIE *(frantic):* No! No one's flying the plane!

INTERIOR: THE COCKPIT

She drags Indiana back into the cockpit, and shows him the empty seats, the mountains ahead of them.

INDIANA: Oh, boy.
WILLIE: They're all gone. Oh, God!

Opposite page: Sketch by Joe Johnston; Production still by Ralph Nelson, Jr.; Special Effects storyboard by Stanley Fleming

Top: Frame enlargement Special Effects storyboard by Stanley Fleming Production still by Ralph Nelson, Jr.

Indy appraises the situation quickly and jumps into the pilot's seat with total confidence.

WILLIE: You know how to fly, don't ya?

Indy surveys the control panels, the myriad dials and switches.

INDIANA: No. *(hopefully)* Do you?

Willie throws her hand over her mouth like she's going to gag with fear.

WILLIE: Oh, no. Oh my God.
INDIANA: How hard can it be?
WILLIE: I'm gonna faint.
INDIANA: Altimeter: okay.
WILLIE *(softly):* I'm gonna faint.
INDIANA: Airspeed: okay. Fuel…fuel…

He taps the fuel gauge and a red light flashes on. The engines sputter.

INDIANA *(continuing):* Fuel!!

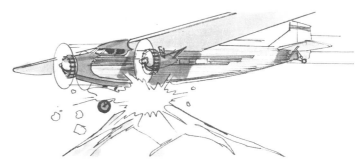

Indiana looks out to see the last engine slow down and quit; all the props are now motionless as the plane noses downward.

INDIANA: I think we got a big problem.

INTERIOR: THE CARGO AREA

Gesturing wildly with his arms, Short Round runs forward.

SHORT ROUND: Dr. Jones!
INDIANA: Shorty!
SHORT ROUND: Dr. Jones, no more parachutes.
INDIANA: Shorty, come on, give me a hand.

They move back into the cargo area.

INTERIOR: THE COCKPIT

Through the windshield Willie sees a huge mountain looming before them. She is paralyzed with fear and can only point at the fast-approaching disaster.

EXTERIOR: THE SKY

The sinking plane smashes some snow off the uppermost pinnacle as it clears a mountain by inches!

INTERIOR: THE CARGO AREA

Top: The Ford Trimotor explodes in a miniature snowbank set. Photo by Terry Chostner
Middle: Stage Coordinator Ed Hirsh prepares the miniature exploding Trimotor set. Photo by Terry Chostner
Bottom: Special Effects storyboard by Stanley Fleming

Willie rushes out of the cockpit and sees Indy pulling some yellow canvas from a storage locker. He gets it out and Willie sees something painted on the side of the canvas:

EMERGENCY LIFE RAFT

Willie is yelling at Indy, very upset.

INDIANA (ignoring her): Shorty, get our stuff.

They drag the folded canvas over to the cargo door.

WILLIE: A boat! We're not sinking, we're crashing!
INDIANA: Grab on, Shorty. Grab on!

Willie sees Short Round rush over to Indiana and grab him around the waist from behind. Willie finally jumps up and runs over.

She throws her arms around Indy's neck so that she and Shorty are both hugging him from behind. Indiana clutches the folded life raft in front of him and surveys the mountainside rushing beneath the sinking airplane.

Finally, an instant before the plane will hit, Indiana dives and pulls the inflation cord! Willie screams.

EXTERIOR: THE SKY

As the plummeting trimotor screams out of control toward the mountain, skimming the rocky snow-covered slopes, we see the life raft spilling out the open door.

The raft pops into its full shape, acting now as a spoiler, soaring against the rushing wind and finally crashing and bouncing against the snowy mountainside.

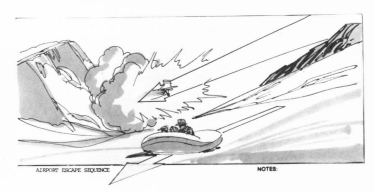

AIRPORT ESCAPE SEQUENCE   NOTES:

Top: Steven Spielberg's sketch for white water storyboard
Production still by Ralph Nelson, Jr.
Special Effects storyboards by Stanley Fleming

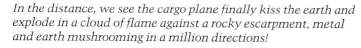

In the distance, we see the cargo plane finally kiss the earth and explode in a cloud of flame against a rocky escarpment, metal and earth mushrooming in a million directions!

EXTERIOR: THE MOUNTAINSIDE

As the raft rockets down the snow, Indiana clutches the front and Willie and Short Round hold on for dear life on either side of him.

SHORT ROUND: Slow it down!

The raft plummets down the mountain, crossing the timberline and slowing down as it scrapes onto bare ground below the snow line.

INDIANA: That wasn't so bad, was it?

He turns and his face turns to panic and all three yell in terror as…

EXTERIOR: A BLUFF

The yellow raft goes airborne over a high cliff and falls endlessly downward until finally it lands with a splash in a raging torrent of white water.

EXTERIOR: WHITE WATER RAPIDS

The raft plunges into the roaring torrent, bouncing over rock-swollen waves, twisting and spinning through narrow gaps. The three helpless passengers are drenched in the thundering cascades of white water.

Willie is hollering, Short Round hangs on wide-eyed, and even Indy looks terrified as the raft crashes down the rapids.

WILLIE: Put on the brakes! I hate the water! And I hate being wet! *(to Indiana)* And I hate you!
INDIANA: Good! Good!

EXTERIOR: RIVER CLEARING

Finally the raft drifts out of the main part of the river and glides toward a clearing. Indy lies back against the side of the raft in relief. Willie topples backward onto the bottom, feet flying upward, as the raft now floats gently on calm water.

INDIANA: All right, Shorty. You okay?
WILLIE: Oh, where are we anyway?

The raft floats to a gentle stop. On the bank above we see a pair of dark legs. Indy squints up into the sun and sees something.

INDIANA: India.
WILLIE: How do you know that?

Short Round gasps as he looks up at the calm, dark face of a SHAMAN. Silhouetted against the blazing sun, the dignified old man in flowing robes stares down at them in the raft.

Willie and Short Round watch mystified as Indiana, in a silent greeting to the old shaman, places his palms together and moves his hands up to touch his forehead.

EXTERIOR: THE MAYAPORE HILLS—DAY

Indiana and Short Round follow the shaman down a gutted path through barren rolling hills. Willie is out of her milieu, stumbling along this forlorn landscape in high heels and Indy's tuxedo, still carrying her lamé gown.

Opposite page: (top right) Executive Producer Frank Marshall (left foreground) with Harrison Ford, Kate Capshaw, and Ke Huy Quan. Photo by Ralph Nelson, Jr.; (left) Production still by Keith Hamshere

Production stills by Keith Hamshere

EXTERIOR: MAYAPORE—DAY

At the base of the hills, the Mayapore village does nothing to relieve the awful sense of devastation. A desolate road runs through the village, along which groups of pitifully poor villagers stare at the strangers being brought in.

Indiana notices the wretched peasants staring at Short Round; one of the women speaks to the little Chinese boy and embraces him. Short Round pulls away nervously.

There is no sign of children in the village and Short Round grows frightened by the odd attention.

EXTERIOR: MAYAPORE VILLAGE—EVENING

Black clouds clot across the sky as darkness begins to fall. Indiana, Willie, and Short Round sit tensely on a shabby rug inside a thatched hut.

The dying sunset silhouettes them and the half-dozen elders seated in the dirt around them. A gray-haired man, the village CHIEFTAIN, gives quiet commands to the women who scuttle in and give wooden bowls to the three visitors. No bowls are placed in front of the elders.

WILLIE: Oh, I sure hope this means dinner. God, I'm starving.

Indiana nods and politely thanks the woman and the chieftain in their own language.

INDIANA *(in Hindi):* Thank you.

Willie looks aghast at the meager, unappetizing food in the bowl.

WILLIE *(quietly):* I can't eat this.
INDIANA: That's more food than these people eat in a week. They're starving.

Willie looks around at the emaciated faces and feels like crawling into a hole.

WILLIE: I'm sorry, you can have my...

She picks up her plate and gently offers it back to the woman.

INDIANA *(to Willie):* Eat it!
WILLIE: I'm not hungry.
INDIANA *(pointedly):* You're insulting them, and you're embarrassing me. Eat it.
SHORT ROUND: Eat it.

27

Director Steven Spielberg with Harrison Ford and camera operator Chic Waterson. Photo by Keith Hamshere.
Special Effects storyboard by Joe Johnston
Right: Matte painting by Chris Evans; Inset, frame enlargement
Bottom: Production painting by Elliot Scott

Willie picks up some food in her fingers, examines it, and gingerly puts it in her mouth. Indiana eats and the villagers move in closer around them as the wind sounds louder through the little hut.

SHORT ROUND *(to Indiana):* Bad news coming. Bad news coming.
INDIANA *(to chieftain):* Can you provide us with a guide to take us to Delhi? I'm a professor. I have to get back to my university.

The chieftain indicates a young villager sitting near them.

CHIEFTAIN: Yes, Sajnu will guide you.
INDIANA: *(Thanks him in Hindi)*

The old shaman speaks now for the first time.

SHAMAN: On the way to Delhi, you will stop at Pankot.
INDIANA *(puzzled):* Pankot is not on the way to Delhi.
SHAMAN: You will go to Pankot Palace.
INDIANA: I thought the palace had been deserted since eighteen fifty...
SHAMAN *(darkly):* No. Now there is new maharajah—and again the palace has the power of the dark light.

The shaman looks around at his unfortunate people.

Opposite page: Production still by Eva Sereny

Below: Production still by Keith Hamshere Right (left to right): Kate Capshaw, Steven Spielberg, Executive Producer George Lucas, and Harrison Ford. Photo by Keith Hamshere

SHAMAN *(continuing):* It is that place kill my people.
INDIANA: What has happened here?
SHAMAN: The evil start in Pankot. Then like monsoon, it moves darkness over all country.

He passes his hand across his eyes.

SHAMAN *(continuing):* Over all of the country.
INDIANA: The evil. What evil?
SHORT ROUND *(to Indiana):* Bad news. You listen to Short Round. You live longer.

Indiana shushes him and the shaman continues with his story.

SHAMAN: They came from palace and took *sivalinga* from our village.

Willie looks over at Indiana.

WILLIE: Took what?

INDIANA: It's a stone. A sacred stone from a shrine that protects the village.
SHAMAN: It is why Shiva brought you here.

The shaman laughs and looks around, enjoying their reaction.

INDIANA *(politely firm):* We weren't brought here. Our plane crashed.
WILLIE *(helpfully):* It crashed.
SHAMAN *(interrupting):* No. No. We prayed to Shiva to help us find the stone. It was Shiva who made you fall from the sky, so you will go to Pankot Palace to find *sivalinga* and bring back to us. Bring back to us.

Indiana's about to object—then he looks at the sad chieftain, the elders and peasants who are watching him helplessly. And he sees again the dark, steady eyes of the old shaman.

EXTERIOR: MAYAPORE VILLAGE

The villagers accompany the shaman, elders, and three visitors out to the edge of the village. Short Round walks beside Indiana.

SHORT ROUND: Dr. Jones, did they make the plane crash? To get you here?
INDIANA: No, Shorty, it's just a ghost story. Don't worry about it.

Short Round looks around as they all stop walking. The shaman motions toward a primitive shrine.

CHIEFTAIN: They took stone from here.

Indiana examines the shrine. In the center of a giant boulder, there is a carved niche. The niche is empty but an indentation indicates the conical shape of the stone that was stolen.

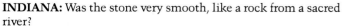
INDIANA: Was the stone very smooth, like a rock from a sacred river?

CHIEFTAIN: Yes.

INDIANA: With three lines across it? *(seeing the chieftain nod)* Representing the three levels of the universe? Yes, I've seen stones like the one you lost. But why would maharajah take the sacred stone from here?

Indy turns again to the old shaman.

SHAMAN: They say we must pray to their evil god. We say we will not.

WILLIE: Excuse me. I don't understand how one rock could destroy a whole village.

The old shaman looks off and fights the tears in his eyes as he starts speaking in Hindi.

INDIANA *(translating):* They say when the sacred stone was taken the village wells dried up and the river turned to sand.

Indy turns and asks the shaman a question in Hindi. The shaman answers in Hindi.

INDIANA *(translating):* The crops were swallowed by the earth. The animals laid down and turned to dust. Then one night there was a fire in the fields. The men went out to fight the fire. When they came back, the women were crying in the darkness.

Indiana asks another question in Hindi and the shaman answers him.

INDIANA *(translating):* Children. He says they stole their children.

EXTERIOR: MAYAPORE VILLAGE—NIGHT

We hear heavy breathing. Above we see the scraggly trees blowing against the full moon as an eerie wind rises and howls. An emaciated boy climbs over rocks through the darkness, going toward the dark village.

EXTERIOR: THE HUT—NIGHT

Leaning against the wall, Indiana hears something, turns, and sees the child in rags running out of the darkness. Indiana moves forward and the child runs toward him. Indy grabs the little boy as he falls into his arms.

Matte painting by Chris Evans
Special Effects storyboard by
Stanley Fleming

The little boy's arm moves and he reaches to Indiana. Indiana takes his small hand and sees that the boy's fingers are cut and bruised. His fingers open and drop something into Indy's hand. The little boy tries to whisper. Indiana has to lean close to hear as the little boy's lips move again.

LITTLE BOY: Sankara…Sankara.

A mother rushes forward now and takes the little boy from Indy's arms. The child's skinny arms go around her as they are reunited. Indiana looks at what the little boy gave him.

It is a small tattered piece of cloth: an old fragment of a miniature painting. Indiana looks at it with an expression of recognition and apprehension.

INDIANA: Sankara….

EXTERIOR: MAYAPORE HILLS—NIGHT

Indiana sits near a tree, staring down at the sleeping village below. Short Round, breathing heavily, climbs up to join him.

SHORT ROUND: The little boy escape from the evil palace. Many other children still there. What we do, Dr. Jones?

Indy stands up, but doesn't respond.

SHORT ROUND *(continuing):* What you think?
INDIANA: I think that somebody believes the good-luck rock from this village is one of the lost Sankara Stones.
SHORT ROUND: What is Sankara?
INDIANA: Fortune and glory, kid. Fortune and glory.

EXTERIOR: THE VILLAGE—MORNING

The camera follows Indiana as he climbs efficiently onto the back of a large elephant. Short Round, mounted on a smaller ele-

33

Above: George Lucas and Steven Spielberg on location in Sri Lanka. Photo by Keith Hamshere Other production stills by Keith Hamshere

phant, grins as Willie makes several futile attempts to climb aboard her mount, aided by two villagers.

INDIANA: Willie, quit monkeyin' around on that thing.

Willie's head comes up over the back of the elephant as she's helped from below. There is a look of sheer terror on her face. She manages to get on, but with her head toward the elephant's rear.

WILLIE *(wailing):* Ohh. Wait a second, Indy. I can't go to Delhi like this!

INDIANA: We're not goin' to Delhi, doll. We're goin' to Pankot Palace.

She looks at Indiana as he rides past.

WILLIE: Pankot?! I can't go to Pankot. I'm a singer!

Sajnu guides her elephant and Willie lurches forward.

WILLIE *(continuing) (yelling):* Oh, I need to call my agent. Is there a phone, anybody? I need a phone.

Indy ignores her hollering. The elephants move off through the crowds of pitiful villagers. Indy sees the elders, the chieftain, and the old shaman, who brings his hands up, as if praying, as Indy rides past.

EXTERIOR: THE COUNTRYSIDE—DAY

The elephants move across the countryside toward the distant hills.

EXTERIOR: THE TRAIL

Indiana rides the lead elephant. Sajnu passes on foot guiding Willie's elephant. With the tuxedo jacket wrapped around her waist, Willie is sniffing the air suspiciously. She sniffs herself, then leans forward and sniffs the elephant, and grimaces.

Willie leans forward and sprinkles perfume on the elephant's head. She yelps when the elephant's trunk comes back, sniffs the foreign fragrance, and suddenly trumpets in disgust.

WILLIE: Oh, quit complaining. This is expensive stuff!

EXTERIOR: LOWER JUNGLES—DAY

Top: Production still by Keith Hamshere
Bottom: Production still by Frank Marshall

From a cliff, we see the elephants below passing into the lower jungles.

Short Round, a little behind the others, speaks confidingly to the baby elephant he's riding.

SHORT ROUND: You come to America with me and we get job in circus. You like that? You like America? You're my best friend.

Indiana and Willie look up and see hundreds of enormous winged creatures flapping across the afternoon sky.

WILLIE: Ooh, what big birds.

Sajnu says something and Indiana nods.

INDIANA: Those aren't big birds, sweetheart. They're giant vampire bats.

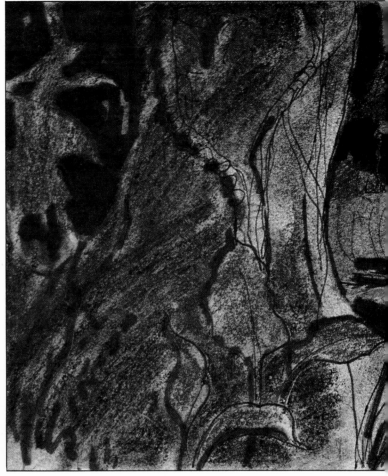

*Production stills by
Keith Hamshere
Production painting by Elliot Scott*

Willie shudders as she watches the bats.
WILLIE *(to herself):* Bats.

EXTERIOR: THE RIVER—LATE
AFTERNOON

An enormous sun silhouettes the three elephants trekking west-ward. Willie drops more perfume on her elephant, both head and rump, ignoring its grunts of protest.

WILLIE: Oh, pipe down, you big baboon. This doesn't hurt. You know what you really need? You really need a bath.

The elephant dips its trunk into the river, flips it backward and shoots a spray of water at Willie. It knocks her off its back and she lands with a splash, sitting in a jungle pool of water, soaked and shocked.

SHORT ROUND *(laughs):* Very funny. Very funny.

Indy moves toward them on his elephant.

SHORT ROUND *(continues to laugh):* Very funny. All wet.

Willie sits in the pool, just about on the edge of tears or hysteria, her voice breaking.

WILLIE: I was happy in Shanghai. I had a little house and a garden. My friends were rich. We went to parties all the time in limousines.

She hits the water with her fists, beginning to sob.

WILLIE *(continuing):* I hate being outside! I'm a singer. *(coughs)* I could lose my voice!

Indiana surveys the area, paying no attention.

INDIANA: I think we'll camp here tonight.

EXTERIOR: RIVER CAMP—NIGHT

On the far side of a campfire, Willie is wrapped in a blanket and shaking out her wet clothes, while Indiana and Short Round sit opposite playing cards. The baby elephant nuzzles Willie's neck with its trunk and she shoves it away impatiently.

WILLIE: Cut it out!
SHORT ROUND *(to Indiana):* Whadda you got?
INDIANA: Two sixes.
SHORT ROUND: Ah, ha! Three aces. I win. Two more game, I have all your money.

He laughs triumphantly.

INDIANA: It's poker, Shorty. Anything can happen.

Willie moves over between them and begins to hang her wet clothes on a tree branch.

WILLIE: So, where did you find your, ah, little bodyguard?
INDIANA: I didn't find him, I caught him.
WILLIE: What?
INDIANA: Shorty's family were killed when the Japanese bombed Shanghai. He's been livin' on the street since he was four. I caught him tryin' to pick my pocket. Didn't I, Short Stuff?

Reaching down for more clothes, Willie comes up instead holding a giant bat by the wings. She screams hysterically. The bat screeches and hisses, flapping its wings in an attempt to get free.

INDIANA *(to Short Round):* The biggest trouble with her is the noise.

Willie runs back and forth past the campfire, continuing to scream, as Short Round and Indiana resume their card game.

SHORT ROUND: Hey, you cheat, Dr. Jones! You cheat. You take four cards.

Willie shrieks again as she comes face to face with a monkey. She races away, only to encounter a huge ugly lizard walking up a tree branch. More screams.

INDIANA *(to Short Round):* Oh, they stuck together.
SHORT ROUND: You pay now! No stuck.
INDIANA: A mistake!
SHORT ROUND: I very little, you cheat very big.

Short Round is getting very angry, and their argument grows more intense. They ignore Willie's continued screaming.

SHORT ROUND: Dr. Jones, you cheat! You pay money. You owe me ten cents.

Indiana grabs Shorty's wrist, and pulls an ace from his sleeve.

INDIANA *(indignant):* Look at this! Look at this! You accuse *me* of cheating!

Short Round breaks out in angry Chinese and Indy responds in Chinese, both of them gesturing and pointing, accusing the other of cheating. Willie's legs race past the campfire, and her screams

*Production stills by
Keith Hamshere*

*Following pages: Matte painting by
Michael Pangrazio; Steven
Spielberg's rough for storyboard
artist Stanley Fleming; the final
Special Effects storyboard is
shown in the upper right hand
corner*

*continue as she runs into an owl, then the lizard again, unable to
find a safe refuge.*

SHORT ROUND *(to Indiana):* You make me poor, no fun. Play
with you no fun.
INDIANA: I quit.

*Short Round answers in Chinese that he quits too and gets up
and stomps away from the campfire. Willie comes running up
and collapses near Indy, exhausted.*

WILLIE: Oh, this place is completely surrounded. The entire
place is crawling with living things.
INDIANA: That's why they call it the jungle, sweetheart.

They hear a low, ominous growl somewhere out in the darkness.

WILLIE: Oh, my God! What else is out there?
INDIANA: Willie, Willie, Willie.

*He touches her shoulder, meaning to be reassuring, but she leaps
up in reaction, screaming again and running to sit on the other
side of the fire.*

INDIANA: Willie, Willie. What is that? Is that short for
something?
WILLIE: Willie is my professional name…Indiana.
SHORT ROUND: Hey, lady. You call him Dr. Jones.
INDIANA: *My* professional name.

He flips a coin to Short Round, who catches it, smiling broadly.

*Willie is sitting on the other side of the fire trying to ignore the
affectionate elephant, which is again nudging her with its trunk.*

WILLIE *(to Indiana):* Why are you dragging us off to this deserted
palace? Fortune and glory?
SHORT ROUND: Fortune and glory.

Indy reaches into his pocket and removes the old piece of cloth given him by the boy in the village and hands it to Willie.

INDIANA: Well…this is a piece of old manuscript. This pictograph represents Sankara. A priest.

The elephant nudges Willie's neck again and she slaps at it.

WILLIE: Scram.
INDIANA: Gently. Gently. This is hundreds of years old.

Willie sees a crude drawing in red, blue, and gold, surrounded by strange hieroglyphics.

WILLIE: Is that some kind of writing?
INDIANA: Yeah, Sanskrit.
WILLIE *(slapping elephant):* Cut it out!

INDIANA: It's part of the legend of Sankara. He climbs Mount Kalisa, where he meets Shiva, the Hindu god.
WILLIE *(examining it):* That's Shiva? And what's he handing the priest?
INDIANA: Rocks. Shiva told him to go forth and combat evil. And to help him he gave him five sacred stones with magical properties.
WILLIE *(looking at Indy):* Magic rocks? My grandpa was a magician. He spent his entire life with a rabbit in his pocket and pigeons up his sleeve. He made a lot of children happy and died a very poor man. Magic rocks. Fortune and glory.

Willie turns away in disgust and sits down by a tree, preparing for bed.

EXT. CASTLE - NIGHT

Low angle of castle at night.
Bats stream forth into the sky.
Full moon in sky.

WILLIE: Sweet dreams, Dr. Jones.
INDIANA: Where you goin'? I'd sleep closer if I were you, for safety's sake.
WILLIE: Dr. Jones, I'd be safer sleeping with a snake.

A real snake's head slithers down from the tree, touching Willie's shoulder. Indiana steps backward, pointing, but unable to speak. Willie thinks it's the elephant again.

WILLIE *(annoyed):* I said, cut it *out!!*

She grabs the snake and gives it a mighty heave into the bushes. Indiana is paralyzed.

WILLIE *(continuing):* I hate that elephant.

EXTERIOR: THE JUNGLE—DAY

Tall, vine-covered trees sway in the wind. Beneath them, the elephants plow through the dense tropical forest. The sounds of the teeming jungle multiply as Short Round surveys the distant hills.

SHORT ROUND *(pointing off in the distance):* Indy, look!
INDIANA: I see it, Shorty. That's it, Pankot Palace.

Willie looks off at the resplendent pinkish-white Moghul-style palace rising in the distance above the jungle. Hundreds of the giant bats fly screeching through the trees overhead.

EXTERIOR: A JUNGLE CLEARING—
LATER

Their Mayapore guide walks toward the camera and suddenly looks frightened. He barks commands and the elephants stop. Indiana climbs down, speaks to the fearful guide, and goes to investigate.

He sees a stone statue of a malevolent goddess with eight arms. Around the goddess's neck hangs a dead bird. Her hands hold carved human heads by their hair.

Indiana moves closer to the statue, fascinated by the ritual objects adorning it: leaves, dead birds, rodents, and turtles. He grimaces as he touches a necklace of real pierced human fingers, and sees that his fingers are wet with blood.

SHORT ROUND *(off screen):* Dr. Jones, what you look at?
INDIANA *(to Short Round):* Don't come up here.

*Opposite page: Matte painting by
Chris Evans and Michael
Pangrazio*

*Matte painting by
Michael Pangrazio
Inset and bottom: Frame
enlargements*

*Matte paintings by
Michael Pangrazio*

*The agitated guides turn the elephants around and start away
with them as fast as possible.*

WILLIE: No, no, no! Oh, Indy! They're stealing our rides.
INDIANA: We walk from here.

*Another cloud of bats passes overhead as the three begin the hike
upward to the palace.*

EXTERIOR: PANKOT PALACE—AFTERNOON

*Indiana and Short Round walk up a rock-paved road beside a
high wall of the palace. Exhausted, Willie trudges along with
them.*

INTERIOR: THE OUTER COURTYARD

Short Round and Willie follow Indiana through a dark archway into a courtyard. The palace seems silent and foreboding. Rajput guards stand at opposite sides of the silent courtyard.

INDIANA: Hello.

A tall, severe-looking Indian in an English suit comes forward to greet them. CHATTAR LAL appraises the intruders with some amusement.

He sees a woozy beauty in a man's tuxedo; a dirty Chinese kid with a baseball cap; a rugged-looking American carrying a bullwhip.

CHATTAR LAL: I should say you look rather lost. But then I cannot imagine where in the world the three of you would look at home.

INDIANA: We're not lost. We're on our way to Delhi. This is Miss Scott. This is Mr. …Round.

SHORT ROUND: Short Round.

INDIANA: My name is Indiana Jones.

CHATTAR LAL *(surprised):* Dr. Jones? The eminent archaeologist?

WILLIE *(sarcastically):* Hard to believe, isn't it?

CHATTAR LAL: Ah, I remember first hearing your name when I was up at Oxford. I am Chattar Lal, Prime Minister to His Highness the Maharajah of Pankot.

INDIANA: Oh.

He and Chattar Lal shake hands, then the Prime Minister turns and bows slightly to Willie, taking her hand.

CHATTAR LAL *(to Willie):* I'm enchanted.
WILLIE *(pleased):* Thank you, very much. Thank you very much.
CHATTAR LAL *(to group):* Welcome to Pankot Palace.

He and Short Round go into the palace and Indiana gestures to Willie to precede him.

INDIANA: Enchanted, huh?

EXTERIOR: PANKOT PALACE—EVENING

Short Round stands on a balcony looking out over the courtyard, as the evening sky grows darker.

INDIANA *(off screen):* Shorty, where's my razor?

INTERIOR: THE PLEASURE PAVILION—
NIGHT

The Pleasure Pavilion is ablaze with torch lights, flickering candles, and exotic music. Female dancers in colorful saris perform on a dais with musicians behind them. Guests in robes and tur-

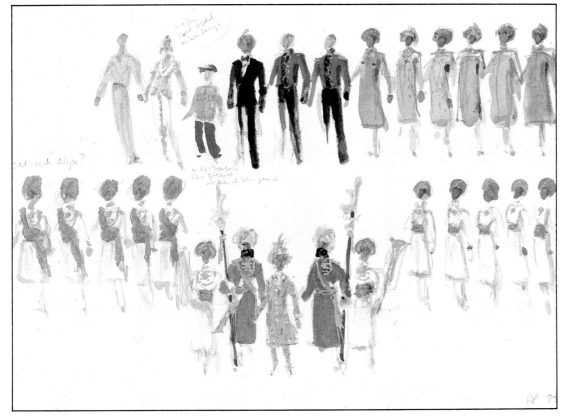

*Opposite page: Production still by
Keith Hamshere*

*Above: Production painting by
Elliot Scott
Costume sketch by
Anthony Powell*

bans stand watching the dancers as Indiana and Chattar Lal enter the room.

CHATTAR LAL: We are fortunate tonight to have so many *unexpected* visitors.

He leads Indiana to join a uniformed British cavalry captain.

CHATTAR LAL *(continuing):* This is Captain Blumburtt.
CAPTAIN BLUMBURTT: Eleventh Puma Rifles. And you, sir, are Dr. Jones, I presume.

Indiana shakes hands with the captain.

INDIANA: I am, Captain.
CHATTAR LAL: Captain Blumburtt and his troops are on a routine inspection tour. The British find it amusing to inspect us at their convenience.
CAPTAIN BLUMBURTT: I do hope, sir, that it is not, ah, inconvenient to you, ah, sir.
CHATTAR LAL: The British worry so about their Empire. Makes us all feel like well-cared-for children.

Short Round comes in, nearly gets run over by the dancers, and escapes, yelling a little Chinese curse. Willie joins them, looking

Costume sketches by Anthony Powell Production still by Keith Hamshere

Opposite page: Costume sketch by Anthony Powell. Production still by Keith Hamshere

Costume sketches by
Anthony Powell
Production stills by
Keith Hamshere

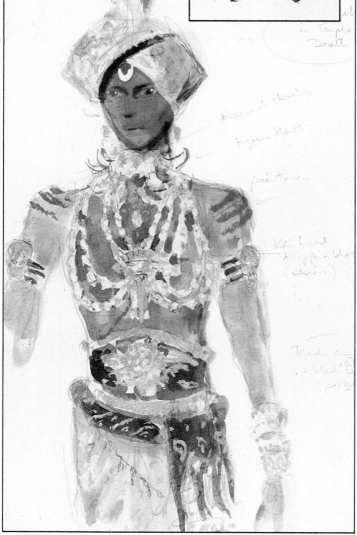

stunning in a gown designed for an Indian princess. She has been loaned some Moghul jewelry, which sparkles on her neck and arms.

INDIANA *(to Willie):* You look beautiful.
WILLIE: I think the maharajah's swimming in loot. Maybe it wasn't such a bad idea coming here, after all.
INDIANA: You look like a princess.
WILLIE *(to Chattar Lal):* Mr. Lal, what do they call the maharajah's wife?
CHATTAR LAL: His Highness has not yet taken a wife.
WILLIE *(happily):* How interesting. Well, ah, maybe it's because he hasn't found the right woman.

As Willie chatters on with the Prime Minister, they move toward the doors of the dining room.

INTERIOR: PLEASURE PAVILION—NIGHT

The assembled guests move toward a long, low table surrounded by colorful pillows. Short Round is next to Willie and Indiana is near the head of the table, across from Chattar Lal.

As everyone stands around the table, Chattar Lal makes an announcement to the guests:

CHATTAR LAL: His Supreme Highness, guardian of Pankot tradition: the Maharajah of Pankot, Zalim Singh.

All eyes are on two solid silver doors, through which now walks the MAHARAJAH ZALIM SINGH. Everyone is bowing, including Indiana and Willie, who looks amazed.

Indeed, Zalim Singh is only thirteen. Outfitted in red-and-gold brocade, festooned with enormous jewels, the little maharajah gazes imperiously at the bowing crowd and finally sits down on golden pillows. He nods, and his guests take their seats.

WILLIE *(to Short Round):* That's the maharajah? A kid!
SHORT ROUND: Maybe he like older women.

Indiana, seated next to Captain Blumburtt, speaks across the table to Chattar Lal.

INDIANA: Captain Blumburtt was just telling me something of the interesting history of the palace, and the importance it played in the mutiny.

CHATTAR LAL: It seems the British never forget the Mutiny of 1857.

INDIANA: Yes, well, you know, I think there are other events before the mutiny, going back a century, back to the time of Clive, that are more interesting.

CHATTAR LAL: And what events are those, Dr. Jones?

INDIANA: If memory serves me correctly, this area, this province, was the center of activity for the Thuggee.

During their conversation, servants have been moving about, preparing for the dinner. They put down a huge platter in front of Willie and Short Round. Willie stares at an enormous steaming boa constrictor on the platter. A fat, turbaned merchant, sitting next to Willie, sighs with pleasure.

MERCHANT: Ah, Snake Surprise.

WILLIE *(aghast):* What's the surprise?

With a flash of a knife, a servant slits *the huge snake and exposes a mass of squirming,* live *baby eels inside.*

Meanwhile, Indiana continues chatting politely with the Prime Minister.

CHATTAR LAL: Dr. Jones, you know perfectly well that the Thuggee cult has been dead for nearly a century.

CAPTAIN BLUMBURTT: Yes, of course. The Thuggee was an obscenity that worshipped Kali with human sacrifices. The British Army nicely did away with them.

Eels are slithering around the table. One of the guests devours them two at a time, with evident relish, although Blumburtt pushes them away distastefully.

INDIANA: Well, I suppose stories of the Thuggee die hard.

CHATTAR LAL: There are no stories anymore.

INDIANA: I'm not so sure. We came from a small village. The peasants there told us Pankot Palace was growing powerful again because of some ancient evil.

Above: Costume sketch by Anthony Powell Production stills by Keith Hamshere

CHATTAR LAL: Village stories, Dr. Jones. They're just…fear and folklore. You're beginning to worry Captain Blumburtt.
CAPTAIN BLUMBURTT *(brushing eel aside):* Not worried, Mr. Prime Minister. Just, ah…just, um, interested.

Servants arrive with platters of the next course: six-inch-long bugs.

Willie whimpers as she watches the fat merchant next to her lift one of the black, shiny baked beetles—and crack it in two! The man proceeds to enthusiastically suck the gooey innards out!

MERCHANT *(looking at Willie):* What, you're not eating?
WILLIE *(weakly):* I…had bugs for lunch.

The merchant chuckles and continues eating.

WILLIE *(to Short Round):* Give me your hat.
SHORT ROUND: Why?
WILLIE: 'Cause I'm gonna puke in it.

Short Round quickly pulls his hat away from her. Meanwhile, Indy continues with the polite but irritated Chattar Lal.

INDIANA: You know, the villagers also told us Pankot Palace had taken something.

CHATTAR LAL: Dr. Jones, in our country, it is not usual for a guest to insult his host.
INDIANA: I'm sorry. I thought we were talking about folkfore.

Willie stops a passing servant, who bends down to her.

PALACE CORRIDOR WITH MIRRO

Opposite page: Production still by Keith Hamshere

Production paintings by Elliot Scott

*Production stills by
Keith Hamshere*

WILLIE: Excuse me, sir, do you have something simple, like soup?
CAPTAIN BLUMBURTT: What exactly was it they say was stolen?
INDIANA: A sacred rock.

Chattar Lal laughs, dismissing the seriousness of Indiana's demeanor.

CHATTAR LAL: You see, Captain. A rock!

The servant returns and places a steaming silver tureen in front of Willie. She perks up, and Short Round leans forward eagerly, holding his spoon ready. Willie breathes in the aroma, then stirs the soup. A dozen eyeballs float to the surface. She screams.

INDIANA *(to Chattar Lal):* Something connected the villagers' rock and the old legend of the Sankara Stones.
CHATTAR LAL: Dr. Jones, we're all vulnerable to vicious rumors. I seem to remember that in Honduras you were accused of being a grave robber rather than an archaeologist.
INDIANA: Well, the newspapers greatly exaggerated the incident.
CHATTAR LAL: And wasn't it the Sultan of Madagascar who threatened to cut your head off if you ever returned to his country?
INDIANA: No, it wasn't my head.
CHATTAR LAL: Then your hands, perhaps?
INDIANA: No, it wasn't my hands. *(chuckles)* It was my, ah…it was a misunderstanding.
CHATTAR LAL: Exactly what we have here, Dr. Jones.
MAHARAJAH: I have heard the evil stories of the Thuggee cult.

When the little maharajah speaks it surprises everyone and there is silence. The maharajah looks at Indiana.

MAHARAJAH *(continuing):* I thought the stories were told to frighten children. Later I learnt the Thuggee cult was once real. And did of unspeakable things. I'm ashamed of what happened here so many years ago. And I assure you, this will never happen again in my kingdom!
INDIANA *(after a moment):* If I offended you, then I am sorry.

Chattar Lal glances at the maharajah and gives him a slight approving nod. Now, more trays are whisked in by servants.

MERCHANT: Ah, dessert!

Willie closes her eyes in dread. But curiosity gets the best of her and she looks—and it's worse than she could imagine:

Plates full of small, dead monkey heads are set in front of each guest. The tops of the monkey skulls have been cut off and sit loose like little covers. Willie watches in utter dismay as the merchant removes the skull top and starts dipping a spoon into what's inside—

MERCHANT *(continuing):* Chilled monkey brains!

Willie keels over, crashing backwards in a dead faint!

INTERIOR: A PALACE HALL—NIGHT

Short Round walks beside Indiana down the shadowy hall toward their room. Short Round carries a cloth-covered dish. The little fellow yawns and shakes his head. They reach their room and Short Round opens the door. Indiana takes the plate from him.

INDIANA: Ah, I think I'll just check on Willie.
SHORT ROUND: That's all you better do. Tell me later what happen.

INDIANA: Am-scray.

Holding the plate behind him, Indy loosens his tie and crosses the hall. As he raises his hand to knock on another door, the door opens and Willie is standing there in pajamas and robe.

INDIANA: Ah, I've got something for you.
WILLIE: There's nothing you have that I could possibly want.
INDIANA: Right.

He turns away and takes a loud bite from an apple. Willie dashes around him, grabs his hands, and greedily attacks the apple.

WILLIE: Oh, you're a very nice man. Maybe you could be my palace slave.

She grabs the plate of fruit and goes into her bedroom, eating happily. Indiana follows. He reaches out and gently touches her necklace. The move is deliberately seductive, and Willie is not displeased.

INDIANA *(smiling):* Wear your jewels to bed, princess?
WILLIE: Yeah—and nothing else. *(smiling)* Shock you?
INDIANA *(shaking his head):* Nothing shocks me. I'm a scientist.

Willie smiles and bites into another apple. Indiana takes off his glasses.

WILLIE: So, as a scientist you do a lot of research?
INDIANA: Always.
WILLIE: What sort of research would you do on me?
INDIANA: Nocturnal activities.
WILLIE: You mean like what sort of cream I put on my face at night, what position I like to sleep in?

He moves closer to her, revealing the passion that's simmering.

INDIANA: Mating customs.
WILLIE: Love rituals?
INDIANA: Primitive sexual practices.
WILLIE: So, you're an authority in that area?
INDIANA: Years of fieldwork.

They move together slowly and kiss hungrily.

WILLIE: I don't blame you for being sore at me. I can be hard to handle.
INDIANA: I've had worse.
WILLIE *(seductively):* But you'll never have better.
INDIANA: I don't know. As a scientist I don't want to prejudice my experiment. I'll let you know in the morning.

Indiana closes the door to the bedroom. A moment later it flies open.

WILLIE *(indignant):* Why, you conceited ape! I'm not that easy!
INDIANA: I'm not that easy either! The trouble with you is, Willie, you're too used to getting your own way.
WILLIE: And you're just too proud to admit that you're crazy about me, Dr. Jones.

Indiana walks across the corridor and opens the door to his own room.

INDIANA: If you want me, Willie, you know where you can find me.

Indy stops by his door and sees Willie smiling as she holds up five fingers.

WILLIE: Five minutes. You'll be back over here in five minutes.
INDIANA: I'll be asleep in five minutes.
WILLIE: Five. You know it, and I know it.

Neither one will surrender first. Willie goes into her room, closing the door. Indy opens his door.

INTERIOR: INDIANA'S SUITE

Indy comes in and closes the door. He sits down on the bed and picks up a clock.

INTERIOR: WILLIE'S SUITE

Willie stands by her door, waiting to hear Indiana walking over. She checks the time on a clock by her bedside.

WILLIE *(to herself):* Five minutes.

INTERIOR: INDIANA'S SUITE

Indiana shrugs and walks over to a couch and starts taking off his tweed jacket and necktie.

INDIANA: Four and a half.

INTERIOR: WILLIE'S SUITE

Willie moves around her lavish suite, turning down lights for romantic effect, checking herself in a mirror.

INTERIOR: INDIANA'S SUITE

Indy checks his reflection in the mirror. The room is magnificently decorated: wall paintings show palace scenes and landscapes; life-sized nautch girls dance, and there are full-scale portraits of Rajput princes on prancing horses. But Indy's more concerned with lust than decor.

INDIANA *(muttering):* Palace slave!

INTERIOR: WILLIE'S SUITE

Lying in bed in a seductive pose, Willie waits for Indy to show up. She starts to look worried. She grabs a clock and shakes it to see if it's working. She paces irritably, wondering if her charm has failed.

WILLIE: Nocturnal activities.

INTERIOR: INDIANA'S SUITE

We see another clock ticking. Indiana paces the room, still muttering.

INDIANA: I'm a conceited ape?!

INTERIOR: WILLIE'S SUITE

WILLIE *(outraged):* "I'll tell you in the morning."

INTERIOR: INDIANA'S SUITE

INDIANA: I can't believe it!

INTERIOR: WILLIE'S SUITE

WILLIE: He's not coming.

INTERIOR: INDIANA'S SUITE

INDIANA: She's not coming. I can't believe I'm not going.

*Production stills by
Keith Hamshere*

*Opposite page: Production
painting by Elliot Scott*

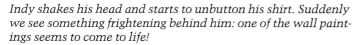
Indy shakes his head and starts to unbutton his shirt. Suddenly we see something frightening behind him: one of the wall paintings seems to come to life!

A large figure in robes and a turban looms out from the wall and lifts a silk cord. The figure wraps the cord suddenly around Indiana's neck! The huge assassin stands behind Indy, twisting the cord even tighter around his neck.

Indy shoves the assassin backwards, ramming the big man into the wall. The assassin maintains his deathgrip—while on the chaise, Short Round sleeps through it all!

Gasping futilely for air, Indy sinks slowly to his knees. Desperately, he grabs a brass pot on the floor by the handle and swings it with his last strength, smashing it up into the assassin's head with a skull-crashing clang!

The assassin is stunned and Indiana curls forward, pulling him into a somersault and sending him flying over his back. The assassin crashes on his spine next to the chaise. Short Round still doesn't wake up.

INTERIOR: PALACE CORRIDOR—NIGHT

Willie's finally had enough waiting and gets out of bed petulantly. She walks across the room and opens the door. She looks out into the empty hall—and shouts defiantly at Indiana's closed door:

WILLIE: Indiana Jones, this is one night you'll never forget. This is the night I slipped right through your fingers.

Across the hall, Indiana fights for his life as Willie goes on with her tirade.

WILLIE *(continuing):* Sleep tight and pleasant dreams! *(suddenly melancholy)* I could've been your greatest adventure.

INTERIOR: INDIANA'S SUITE

As Indy continues his desperate struggle to loosen the assassin's deadly grip, a lamp is kicked over and crashes to the floor. Short Round stirs slightly—then pulls his hat down over his eyes, still unaware that Indy is battling for his life as Shorty peacefully sleeps on.

More objects crash to the floor, and Short Round, finally awakened by the noise, sits bolt upright on the bed. Always Indy's protector, he instinctively leaps to his feet, grabs Indy's whip, and tosses it to him just as Indy begins to gain the upper hand.

SHORT ROUND: Doctor Jones! Your whip!

Indiana grabs his whip, rolls, and lands on his feet. As the assassin tries to retreat, Indy unleashes his whip. It CRACKS and wraps around the killer's neck.

The big man struggles, pulling on the whip, trying to release it from his throat—and Indiana holds fast, watching the killer gasping for air now as his face turns red.

Suddenly the assassin does a full-blown backwards somersault, which rips the whip out of Indy's hand. The assassin has an instant to grin victoriously…

Until he sees that the whip handle is arching toward the ceiling, where it gets caught on the revolving fan! The surprised assassin is tugged upwards…and the whip twists around the ceiling fan like fishing line around a fishing reel.

And like a doomed flounder, the assassin is slowly reeled in and dragged toward the ceiling, his toes lifting off the marble floor. The assassin gasps as he is hanged!

Short Round spins a 360° turn, then looks up as the assassin's legs spin round and round. He shuts his eyes to the grisly sight.

INDIANA *(off screen):* Shorty.

Short Round opens his eyes.

INDIANA: Turn off the switch.

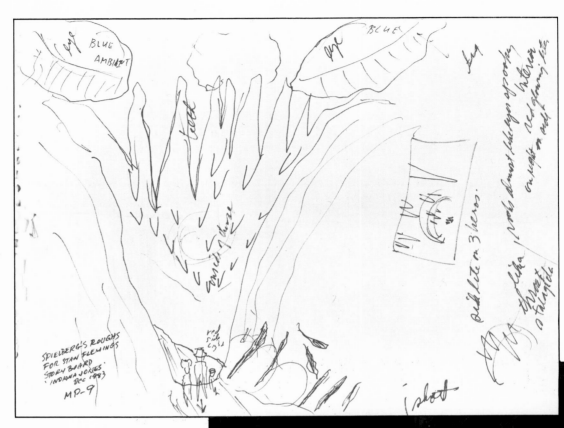

Steven Spielberg sketch for
storyboard artist Stanley
Fleming. Final Special Effects
storyboard below
Matte painting by Frank Ordaz

INT. CAVE

Indy, Willy & Shorty come toward camera at a
slight 3/4 angle.

NOTES:

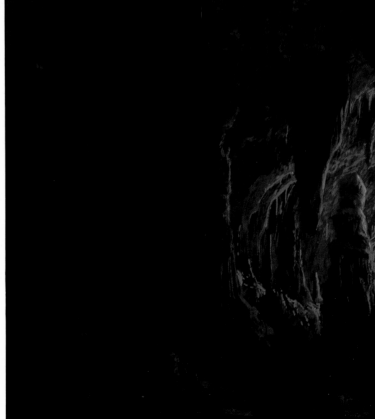

Shorty goes over and turns off the fan. The assassin's body drops,
and Indy recoils his whip. Indy rushes across the hall to Willie's
suite.

INTERIOR: WILLIE'S SUITE

The door bursts open and Indiana rushes in looking around for
the assassin's means of entry. Willie sits up in bed, believing he's
there for another purpose.

WILLIE: Oh, Indy. Be gentle with me.

He comes toward the bed, and Willie crawls on hands and knees
to meet him.

WILLIE (continuing): Be gentle with me.

Now he searches under the bed, apparently not seeing her.

WILLIE: I'm here.

Indiana checks the grillwork on the window, walking the perimeter of the room.

INDIANA: There's nobody here.
WILLIE: No, *I'm* here. Indy, you're acting awfully strange.

In his search, Indy feels a slight breeze that moves a vase of dried flowers. He checks the source, running his hands over a carved stone figure of a woman. His hands rest on her breasts.

WILLIE: Hey, I'm right here.

Indiana shoves the statue. It slides back, revealing the opening of a passage and a painted inscription on the wall.

Indy peers into the tunnel at the old wall painting. Spidery Sanskrit calligraphy runs under a flaking illustration of a priest bowing before a god.

INDIANA *(He reads aloud an inscription in Sanskrit):* "Follow the footsteps of Shiva. Do not betray his truth."

Indy takes out the piece of cloth the boy gave him in Mayapore;

the similarities are striking. It is also a picture of Shiva and Sankara.

Short Round enters Willie's room as Indy calls out to him.

INDIANA: Shorty, go get our stuff.

Willie watches, bewildered, as Short Round runs to obey Indiana.

INTERIOR: A PALACE TUNNEL—NIGHT

Indiana and Short Round enter the secret passage and move forward slowly into the inky darkness.

INDIANA: Stay behind me, Short Round. Step where I step. And don't touch anything.

Exploring, Short Round sees a metal ring on the wall and immediately pulls it. The door shatters and two mummified corpses fall out on him. He yells. Indiana helps him up.

SHORT ROUND: I step where you step. I touch nothing!

INTERIOR: WILLIE'S SUITE

*Production stills by
Keith Hamshere*

Willie paces the room in frustration. She hits the wall near the entrance to the passage.

WILLIE: Indy!

Finding another carving of a woman, she pushes at it tentatively, expecting another passage to open. Nothing.

INTERIOR: THE TUNNEL

Short Round and Indiana creep slowly down the dark tunnel. It grows smaller, and Indiana ducks his head.

SHORT ROUND: I step on something.

Their footsteps crunch on the tunnel floor.

INDIANA: Yeah, there's something on the ground.
SHORT ROUND: Feel like I step on fortune cookies.
INDIANA: It's not fortune cookies. Let me take a look.

Indiana gets a match out of his pocket. He snaps it with his thumb and the match flares. They freeze as the light illuminates a grisly scene:

The floor and walls of the narrow tunnel are an undulating mass of millions of enormous bugs, a hideous insectarium: a living collection of the world's ugliest arthropods, hexapods, and arachnids. A scorpion crawls on Short Round's leg.

SHORT ROUND: That's no cookie!
INDIANA: It's all right. I got it.

Indiana turns and sees something else as the match burns out.

INDIANA: Ow. Go. There. Go.

60

Short Round happily scampers into the chamber and Indy follows him. Short Round unwittingly steps on a button on the floor and suddenly the stone door rolls shut. Another door, opposite, rumbles closed, trapping them inside!

INTERIOR: THE CHAMBER

Indiana strikes a match and lights some cloth covering two skeletons on the floor of the chamber. Short Round starts toward him.

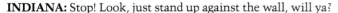

INDIANA: Stop! Look, just stand up against the wall, will ya?

Obediently, Short Round leans back against the wall, hands in his pockets. A block of stone behind him moves under the pressure, and with an ominous rumble, the ceiling begins to descend.

SHORT ROUND *(loudly):* You say to stand against the wall! I listen to what you say! Not my fault! Not my fault.
INDIANA *(hollering):* Willie, get down here! Willie!

INTERIOR: WILLIE'S SUITE

She hears Indiana calling her from the secret passage.

INDIANA *(off screen):* Willie!

Grumbling, Willie pulls on her robe and picks up a lamp.

WILLIE: I bet I get all dirty again.

INTERIOR: THE CHAMBER

The ceiling continues to move slowly downward and Short Round continues to deny responsibility.

SHORT ROUND: That not my fault!
INDIANA *(hollering):* Willie, come down here! We're in trouble!!

Willie is frightened and confused, just entering the passage and carrying the oil lamp.

WILLIE: Trouble, what sort of—

She screams as she runs across the two mummies in the tunnel.

INTERIOR: THE CHAMBER

A skeleton on the floor jerks upright as deadly spikes punch up through the floor and start down from the ceiling. Indy and Short Round start pounding on the door and shout.

INDIANA *(shouting):* This is serious.

INTERIOR: THE TUNNEL

Willie is staring horrified at the two corpses on the wall.

WILLIE: There're two *dead* people down here!
INDIANA *(off screen):* There are gonna be two dead people in *here!* Hurry!

Holding the lamp, Willie starts into the tunnel.

Production stills by Keith Hamshere

WILLIE: I've almost had enough of you two!

INTERIOR: THE SPIKE CHAMBER

Indiana desperately tries to pry the door open with a rock.

INDIANA: Willie!

INTERIOR: THE TUNNEL

Willie moves forward into the tunnel, and we see the bugs scuttling on the floor and walls.

WILLIE: What's the rush?

INTERIOR: THE CHAMBER

The spikes are moving inexorably closer to the two trapped figures.

INDIANA: It's a long story, Willie. Hurry or you don't get to hear it!

INTERIOR: THE TUNNEL

As Willie moves forward, there is the sound of bugs crunching underfoot.

WILLIE: Oooh, God, what is this? Indy! What is this? I can't see a thing.

INTERIOR: THE CHAMBER

Indiana, desperate, puts his hand against the ceiling, trying to stop or slow its descent. Short Round is clinging to his back, terrified.

INDIANA: Hurry!

INTERIOR: THE TUNNEL

Willie strikes a match, holding it up to see what's around her.

WILLIE: Oh, all right. Oh…I broke a nail.

She turns her hand over to examine the nail and sees—a huge bug crawling on her palm. She screams.

INTERIOR: THE CHAMBER

SHORT ROUND: Willie, hurry!

Indiana wedges a skull between the wall and ceiling, but the spikes keep on coming.

INTERIOR: THE TUNNEL

WILLIE *(offscreen):* They're in my hair!
INDIANA: Ah, shut up, Willie!

She is nearly at the door of the spike chamber now, covered with creeping bugs, and frantic.

WILLIE: *(offscreen):* Indy, let me in!
SHORT ROUND: No, let us out!

*Costume sketches by
Anthony Powell*

WILLIE: Let me in!
SHORT ROUND: Let us out!
INDIANA: Shut up!

Willie has arrived outside the door of the chamber.

WILLIE: Let me in. They're all over me!
INDIANA: There's gotta be a fulcrum release lever somewhere.
WILLIE: What?
INDIANA: A handle that opens the door! Go on, look!

Willie whines and frantically searches the door. Insects are crawling and jumping on her and she brushes at them.

WILLIE: There's no handle, just two square holes.
INDIANA *(offscreen):* Go to the right hole!
SHORT ROUND: Hurry, Willie!

Willie moans, and reluctantly reaches her hand into the hole on the left. She shrieks as Indiana's hand suddenly appears and grabs her wrist.

INDIANA: The other one! The other right! *Your* other right! The one on your right!

The hole on the right is revolting, covered with squirming insects. It also oozes some kind of glistening mucus.

WILLIE: Oooh, there's slime inside! I can't do it.
INDIANA: You can do it. Feel inside!
WILLIE: Okay.

She moves her hand toward the nauseating hole, then pulls back.

WILLIE: *(continuing):* You feel inside.
INDIANA: *Do it now.*
WILLIE *(screams):* Okay!

INTERIOR: SPIKE CHAMBER

63

Indiana turns his head sideways and sucks in his breath, but the deadly spikes are nearly poking into his leather jacket now. One presses down the brim of his hat.

INDIANA: *We are going to die!*

INTERIOR: THE TUNNEL

Willie reaches her hand into the disgusting hole, pushing through bugs to search for the release lever. Her face is turned away from the awful door.

WILLIE: It's soft. It's moving!

Her hand touches the lever, then grasps it and pulls.

WILLIE: Got it!

INTERIOR: THE SPIKE CHAMBER

Opposite page: Production painting by Elliot Scott

Near right: A Steven Spielberg sketch suggesting the characteristics of Mola Ram Above: Further development of Mola Ram, sketch by Anthony Powell

The spikes suddenly retract, disappearing into the floor and ceiling, and the stone door slides back into the wall. Short Round jumps up, but Indy remains squatting on the floor, glaring at Willie as she runs frantically into the chamber.

WILLIE: Get 'em off of me. Get 'em off of me! They're all over me! Get 'em off! They're all over my body!

She jumps up and down trying to shake off the insects that are all over her. She bends to brush at her legs, and her buttocks strike the stone block that triggers the trap. With a rumble, the door rolls back again, sealing the doorway, and the spikes begin to appear all over again.

SHORT ROUND: It wasn't me! It was her!

Willie screams and Short Round points to the rapidly closing doorway on the opposite side of the chamber.

SHORT ROUND: Come on! Get out!

They race for the doorway.

INDIANA: Go! Move! Come on!

Everyone gets out just in the nick of time, and in the final moment before the stone doorway crashes shut, Indiana's hand reaches back and grabs his hat.

INTERIOR: THE WIND TUNNEL

Indiana, Short Round, and Willie exit the spike chamber and start down a larger tunnel through which a roaring wind intermittently blows, howling eerily like a note of gloomy music.

Indiana follows a curve in the tunnel, and they see light ahead. The wind howls another dramatic note that gales past them as they reach the mouth of the tunnel.

They all stare in astonishment at the sight below them:

CAMERA CONTINUES TO TILT UP AS APPROACHING FIGURE BREAKS INTO LIGHT.

INTERIOR: THE TEMPLE OF DOOM

As the camera pulls back, the mouth of the wind tunnel in which they are standing becomes just a small hole overlooking the staggering vastness of the incredible TEMPLE OF DOOM.

The colossal subterranean temple has been carved out of a solid mass of rock. A vaulting cathedral-like ceiling is supported by rows of carved stone columns.

Balconies overlook the temple floor. Pillared halls lead off to dark side chambers. Mammoth stone statues of elephants, lions and demigods (half/man half/animal monstrosities) loom above the crowds of chanting worshippers.

The altar is a platform jutting out from the stone wall of the cavern. Separating the worshippers from this altar is a natural crevasse, out of which wisps of smoke rise occasionally.

INTERIOR: THE ALTAR

On the other side of the crevasse, evil-looking priests in robes materialize out of clouds of swirling smoke. The priests carry smoke-billowing urns to a giant stone statue.

Now we see the hideous protectress of the temple, the obscenely malevolent object of the cult's devotion: the bloodthirsty goddess KALI!

The priests bow at the base of the statue and gaze up reverently at their Kali Ma. Skulls surround her stone feet, carved serpents twist up her legs, while around her waist there is a gruesome belt of human hands.

In one of her four arms, she holds a sword; in the second, the severed head of a giant. With her other hands, she encourages her worshippers, who are chanting louder and louder!

Kali's face is loathsome: her earrings are two corpses. Her evil tongue extends out of her twisted mouth, and what looks like real blood flows over her long fangs and down her naked breasts.

Opposite page: Production still by Keith Hamshere

Top and bottom: Storyboards by Andrew G. Probert
Middle: Storyboards by Edward Verreaux

CAMERA CONTINUES TO PUSH IN TO A THREE-SHOT. CAMERA CRANES DOWN & TILTS UP.
3 MEN TURN TOWARD US AND BEAT THEIR DRUMS 3 TIMES.

Opposite page: Production stills by
Keith Hamshere

Production still by
Keith Hamshere
Storyboards by Andrew G. Probert

HE THEN RAISES HIS RIGHT HAND AND ARCS IT TO THE RIGHT — THE CAMERA FOLLOW.

MOLA RAM TURNS TO LOOK AT CAMERA — THEN TO THE RIGHT. (HIS LEFT)

VICTIM — TOWARD CAMERA.

WE PAN UP TO STATUE — IRON GRILL IS DESCENDING — CLICK, CLICK. WE FOLLOW IT DOWN.

MOLA RAM RAISES HIS HAND SLOWLY INTO THE AIR.

68

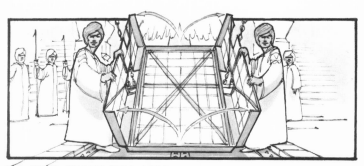

TWO GUARDS OPEN THE GRILL'S DOORS.

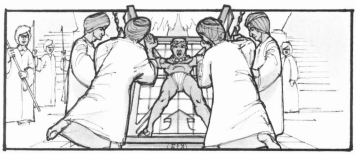

VICTIM IS PLACED INTO GRILL.

A SLIVER OF LIGHT OPENS ACROSS VICTIM.

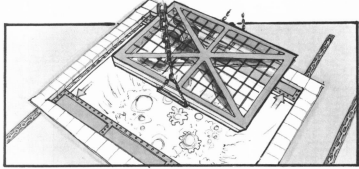

DOORS - OPENING CONTINUES .

INTERIOR: THE WIND TUNNEL

Indiana, Willie, and Short Round look down at the mystery cult in the temple.

INDIANA: It's a Thuggee ceremony. They're worshipping Kali.
WILLIE: Have you ever seen anything like this before?
INDIANA: Nobody's seen this for a hundred years.

INTERIOR: THE TEMPLE OF DOOM

A huge drum sounds three times, and the chanting stops. The silence is chilling as another robed figure appears out of the smoke on the altar.

This is MOLA RAM, the High Priest of the Thuggee cult. Mola Ram's red-rimmed eyes glare from the sunken sockets in his pale, sinister face. Here is a man who looks as vile and diabolical as the unholy goddess rising behind him.

As the drum booms three times more, Mola Ram lifts his hand, and suddenly there is a scream.

All heads turn toward an unfortunate, struggling Indian being dragged out by priests. The man screams again as he's locked into an upright iron frame.

Mola Ram steps forward to his victim, and the man looks up into the High Priest's grotesque face. Mola Ram begins a ritual chant in Sanskrit as his hand moves almost caressingly across the man's face and neck.

Suddenly, Mola Ram's hand shoots out toward the man's chest— and pierces it! The High Priest's hand sinks into the victim's writhing body and rips out his living heart!

INTERIOR: THE WIND TUNNEL

Willie screams in absolute horror and begins to hyperventilate.

INDIANA *(to himself):* He's still alive.

*Storyboards by Andrew G. Probert
Lower left: Stop-motion animator Tom St. Amand sculpts a figure to be used for miniature effects shots. Photo by Kerry Nordquist
Lower right: A miniature puppet is lowered into the lava pit set. Photo by Kerry Nordquist*

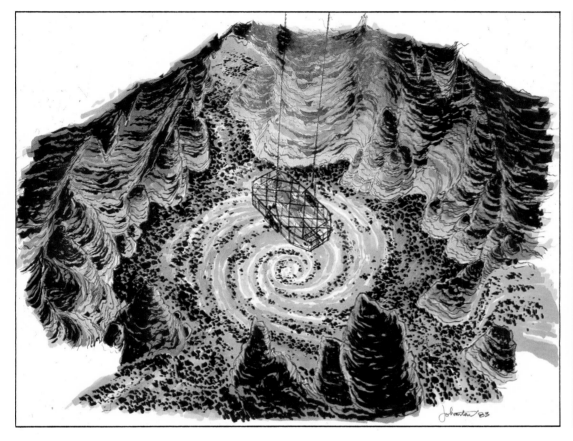

INTERIOR: THE ALTAR

Indeed, the bloody heart is *still beating in Mola Ram's hand! He lifts the heart into the air, and the worshippers begin to chant.*

THE MULTITUDE: *Jai ma Kali, jai ma Kali!*

Stranger still, the sacrificial victim looks down at his chest and realizes he is still alive; there is no evidence of a gash on his chest, only a reddish mark.

The man thrashes about helplessly on the iron frame as it is upended and the heavy stone doors below him are opened, emitting intense heat and a rush of steam from the pit below.

As the sacrificial victim looks down into the crevasse below him, he screams—and we see the molten lava bubbling crimson at the bottom of the chasm! The priests slowly release the lever, and the victim descends into the mouth of Hell.

INTERIOR: THE WIND TUNNEL

Willie, her back to the Temple, closes her eyes but Indy and Short Round watch horrified as the iron frame is lowered—and the bloody heart continues to beat in Mola Ram's hand—and the molten lava burns and flares as the screaming victim is lowered deeper into the crevasse.

INTERIOR: THE TEMPLE

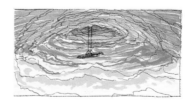

Above, right: The lava pit on the ILM stage. Photo by Kerry Nordquist Sketches by Joe Johnston

The man's skin blisters as he's lowered within feet of the lava. His flesh smokes and he screams one last time as his hair bursts into flame.

The iron frame sinks and submerges into the boiling fiery lava...

INTERIOR: THE ALTAR

Above the crevasse, Mola Ram continues to hold the heart up in his hand. The heart is smoking and dripping blood. It beats faster, bursts into flames—and disappears!

INTERIOR: THE TEMPLE

The iron frame is raised out of the lava. The metal glows red like a branding iron, but there is no trace of the sacrificial victim.

INTERIOR: THE WIND TUNNEL

As the wind howls again, Willie and Short Round look sickened and appalled by the ceremony. Even Indy seems shaken by what they are witnessing.

THE MULTITUDE: *Jai ma Kali, jai ma Kali!*

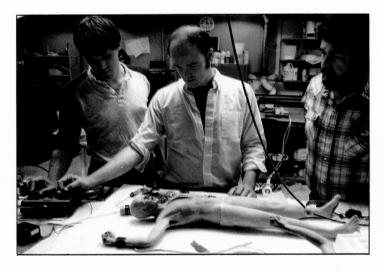

Above: AT ILM, Effects Art Director Joe Johnston, Creative Consultant Phil Tippett and Model Maker Ira Keeler check remote control movements on a miniature puppet. Photo by Terry Chostner
Near right: The lava pit set at ILM
Far right: Paul Huston creates turbulence in the glycerine whirlpool at the bottom of the set. Photos by Kerry Nordquist

INTERIOR: THE ALTAR

Mola Ram walks back past the altar and disappears. Behind him, three priests carry cloth-wrapped objects toward the altar.

The priests reverently unwrap three conical pieces of crystallized quartz. They place the three stones in the eyes and mouth of the skull below the statue of Kali. As the stones are brought together, they start to glow a burning incandescent white.

INTERIOR: THE WIND TUNNEL

Short Round looks scared. Willie is still crying. Indy watches, horrified but fascinated.

INDIANA: That's the rock they took from the village. It's one of the Sankara Stones.
SHORT ROUND: Why they glow like that?
INDIANA: Shh. The legend says when the rocks are brought together, the *diamonds* inside them will glow.
SHORT ROUND: Diamonds?
WILLIE *(whispers):* Diamonds.
SHORT ROUND: Diamonds!

Willie wipes her eyes and becomes more interested.

WILLIE: *Diamonds...*

Indiana shushes them both. As the wind howls about them, Indiana and Willie stare at the glowing stones, seduced by different aspects of their legend.

INTERIOR: THE ALTAR

Left: Dave Sosalla constructs a chest replica that will be used in the human sacrifice shot. Photo by Kerry Nordquist
Right: The moveable armature that will be inside the latex foam puppet allowing the body movements required for stop motion animation. Photo by Kerry Nordquist

The Sankara Stones shimmer brightly, and inside the crystallized quartz, the enormous sparkling diamonds of legend are now revealed.

INTERIOR: THE WIND TUNNEL

Indiana sees the worshippers below start to leave the temple. He looks at Willie and Short Round.

INDIANA: Hey, hey. Look, I want you two to stay up here and keep quiet. Shorty, you keep an eye on her.

Short Round nods. Willie sees Indiana peering down at the sheer drop below the mouth of the wind tunnel.

WILLIE: Why? Where are you going?
INDIANA: Down there.
WILLIE: Down there?! Are you crazy?
INDIANA: I'm not leaving here without the stones.
WILLIE: You could get killed chasing after your damn fortune and glory!
INDIANA (looking at her): Maybe…(smiling) But not today.

Indiana kisses her and looks down at the now empty temple. Then he slips down from the mouth of the tunnel.

INTERIOR: THE BALCONY

Indiana walks quietly along the balcony overlooking the temple. He stops: between him and the altar is the crevasse with the lava bubbling fire at the bottom. Indiana looks across the gulf and sees another column near the altar at the top of which stone elephants are perched. Indy uncurls his whip and suddenly lets it fly.

The whip cracks and its end wraps tightly around the overhanging column. From the balcony, Indy tugs the whip taut, takes a breath, and runs—

INTERIOR: THE CREVASSE

Indiana leaps and swings out on the whip, arching down and up and over the chasm of fiery lava in a spectacular curving jump!

INTERIOR: THE ALTAR

Indiana lands on his feet and turns to release the whip. Recurling the whip, Indy attaches it to his belt and moves toward the towering statue of Kali. The three Sankara Stones still glow, and Indiana approaches them cautiously.

Suspiciously, Indiana touches the stone, but it doesn't burn. He lifts it carefully and peers into it, its glow reflecting on his face. The diamond glow fades as he places the stone in his shoulder bag and reaches for the others.

INTERIOR: THE WIND TUNNEL

Short Round and Willie watch apprehensively as Indiana bags the three stones.

INTERIOR: THE ALTAR

Indiana backs away and looks up at the horrific statue of Kali. It seems to be watching him. He turns and is about to go when he hears something.

It sounds like a voice and Indy is afraid to turn—could it be Kali? Then he hears other noises echoing and turns slowly. Realizing the sounds are coming from behind the altar, Indy moves around it toward the back.

INTERIOR: THE WIND TUNNEL

Short Round and Willie are mystified as they see Indiana disappear behind the altar.

WILLIE: Where's he going?

Short Round and Willie scream in shock as a huge Thuggee guard suddenly appears in front of them! He grabs at Short Round, who struggles madly in the man's grasp.

SHORT ROUND: Run, Willie, run!

INTERIOR: CHAMBER BEHIND ALTAR

Opposite page: Storyboards by Edward Verreaux; Production still by Keith Hamshere

Top: Special Effects storyboard by Phill Norwood Production still by Keith Hamshere Bottom: storyboard by Edward Verreaux

Indiana enters the dark chamber behind the altar. The only illumination is the light streaming out from around the silhouetted statue of Kali.

Indy slowly moves toward a cylindrical shaft of light rising up from what appears to be an enormous hole.

Indy hears voices and the clink of metal against rock as he continues forward. The ground is dark in front of the large hole. He edges toward the precipice and the light rising up illuminates the look of shock on his face as he peers down into Hell.

INTERIOR: THE THUGGEE MINES

Indy looks into a deep pit around which concentric paths lead off into numerous narrow tunnels. Crawling out of these burrows, scrawny children drag sacks of dirt and rock. Other hollow-eyed children pull sacks to mine cars waiting on rails.

Straining to lift the rocks into the mine cars, several of the children slip and fall. Bare-chested Thuggee guards shout at the enslaved children and kick those who've fallen.

For these children there would seem to be only one hope: death—an end to their travail.

Indiana edges around the hole, looking into the ghastly mine and feeling as if he's discovered an inferno of misery as grotesque as Dante's.

Indy shifts the bag of stones on his shoulder. He hesitates and considers his choice: he has the Sankara Stones and can leave with them now....

But Indiana hears the pleading cries of one child and peers down to see a burly Thuggee guard raise his arm and bring it down to the pitiful little slave. Indy gets angrier and angrier as he watches.

He grabs a rock. He lifts it and flings it down into the mine.

INTERIOR: THE MINE

We see Indiana above and the rock hurtling down. It crashes onto the shoulder of the giant Thuggee guard and bounces off.

*Costume sketches by
Anthony Powell*

*Opposite page: Production
still by Keith Hamshere; Costume
sketch by Anthony Powell*

INTERIOR: THE CHAMBER

*Indy sees the startled slave children looking up at him in shock.
He smiles victoriously at the Thuggee below, who looks up to
see what has happened. The smile fades as he turns and sees
behind him at least a dozen of the weirdly painted temple guards
with knives drawn.*

INTERIOR: A CELL—NIGHT

*Indiana is shoved into a barred cell, and his hands are chained
above his head. In the murky light, he sees Short Round sitting in
chains across the cell.*

SHORT ROUND: Dr. Jones!

76

He runs over and hugs Indy.

SHORT ROUND: I keep telling you, you listen me more, you live longer.

Indiana nods groggily. He sees a young boy in rags sitting near Short Round. Through the iron bars of the cell, Indy sees the children slaving in the mine tunnels.

BOY: Please let me die. I pray to Shiva let me die, but I do not. Now, now the evil of Kali take me.
SHORT ROUND: How?
BOY: They will make me drink the blood of the Kali. Then I'll fall into the black sleep of the Kali Ma.
INDIANA: What is that?
BOY: You become like them. We'll be alive—but like a nightmare. You drink blood, you not wake up from nightmare.

The boy cowers in the darkness at the back of the cell, like a trapped animal awaiting the inevitable.

INTERIOR: MOLA RAM'S CHAMBER

Indiana is chained to a rock inside the chamber. It is a terrifying gallery of ritualistic statues and grisly icons of the evil Thuggee sect.

In a corner there is another statue of Kali herself, draped with flowers, necklaces of real human skulls, and slithering belts of live snakes.

Fresh blood has been splashed over the statue, and at its base are the three Sankara Stones recovered from Indiana. Mola Ram walks over to stand before him.

MOLA RAM: You were caught trying to steal the Sankara Stones.

Mola Ram gazes transfixed at the stones glowing on the altar.

MOLA RAM *(continuing):* There were five stones in the beginning. Over the centuries they were dispersed by wars. Sold off by thieves like you.
INDIANA: Thieves like me, huh? Ha! You're still missing two.
MOLA RAM: A century ago when the British raided this temple and butchered my people, a loyal priest hid the last two stones down here in the catacombs.

INDIANA: So, that's what you've got these *slaves* digging for, huh? They're innocent children.

Short Round is held by a guard near the wall, and Mola Ram puts his hand on the boy's head, caressingly.

MOLA RAM: They dig for the gems to support our cause. They also search for the last two stones. Soon we will have all the five Sankara Stones, and the Thuggee will be all-powerful!
INDIANA: What a vivid imagination.
MOLA RAM *(chuckles):* You don't believe me? You will, Dr. Jones. You will become a true believer.

The giant Thuggee guard from the mines comes in and walks over to Indiana, towering above him.

INDIANA: Hi.

The boy from the cell enters, now dressed as a Thuggee guard. He walks forward, zombielike, and hands Mola Ram a human skull full of blood. The guard holds Indiana's head back and forces his mouth open. Mola Ram tips the skull and blood spills out of its death-grinning jaws and flows into Indiana's mouth. Indy gags.

SHORT ROUND: Dr. Jones, don't drink! It's bad! Don't drink! Spit it out!

Opposite page: (top) Production still by Keith Hamshere; (bottom) The miniature animation puppets created by Creative Consultant Phil Tippett, Stop Motion Animator Tom St. Amand, and Stop Motion Technician Dave Sosalla. Photo by Kerry Nordquist

Production stills by Keith Hamshere

Suddenly Indiana spits the blood, spraying Mola Ram and the guard. Looking at his blood-spattered clothes, Mola Ram is furious. He turns and speaks to the little maharajah, who walks forward.

The little prince's eyes glow angrily and he hisses at Indy, then pulls a small krtya *from his robes. The doll has been crudely fashioned to resemble Indiana. The maharajah turns and sticks the doll into a flaming urn. Indiana suddenly cries out and twists in pain as he is burned! The little prince smiles evilly.*

SHORT ROUND *(shouts in Chinese):* Dr. Jones!

Suddenly Short Round karate kicks the maharajah, knocking him and the krtya to the ground. But his fight is cut off as the guards recapture him and chain him with his hands above his head.

The guards roughly turn Indiana around and chain him with his face against the rock. The giant Thuggee picks up the bullwhip. Mola Ram stands, splattered with blood, holding the skull cup in his hands.

MOLA RAM *(to Indiana):* You dare not do that.

He gives orders to the guard. Indiana jerks as the bullwhip rips through his shirt and tears open his flesh. At the side, the maharajah whips Short Round, who seems stunned, then yells in pain.

INDIANA: Leave him alone, you bastards!

The guard whips Indiana twice again, and then forces his head far back, holding Indy's mouth open. Mola Ram lifts the skull again toward Indiana's mouth.

Production still by
Keith Hamshere
Storyboards by Andrew G. Probert

MOLA RAM: The British in India will be slaughtered. Then we will overrun the Moslems. Then the Hebrew god will fall.

Indiana's head is held back and Mola Ram spills the blood. It flows out of the mouth of the skull and into Indy's mouth.

MOLA RAM *(continuing):* Then the Christian god will be cast down and forgotten.

Indy's eyes look horrified as the blood flows from the skull down his choking throat. The guard pinches his nose and mouth closed, and Indiana is forced to swallow.

MOLA RAM: Soon Kali Ma will rule the world.

Indiana coughs, held up helplessly by the guard. Short Round watches with tears in his eyes.

SHORT ROUND *(whispers):* Dr. Jones.

INTERIOR: CATACOMBS—NIGHT

Indiana lies on a rough stone slab, surrounded by hundreds and hundreds of candles. His hands and body convulse, and he groans in pain as the unspeakable potion takes effect. Suddenly his body relaxes. He raises his hand to examine it in wonder, smiles strangely, and then laughs.

INTERIOR: MINE TUNNELS—NIGHT

Beneath the temple, down in the bowels of the mountain, the pitiful children dig at the earth with their fingers. A FAT GUARD slouches down the tunnel, flogging malingerers with a leather strap.

Short Round sweats next to the others, clawing at the rocks, doomed to work with them now in their search for the last two Sankara Stones.

The leather strap suddenly flays Short Round's back and he barely manages not to scream out in pain. The fat guard passes. Short Round grabs a large rock and smashes it down on the leg chains binding him. Shorty beats at the chain with the rock, determined to escape.

GUARD TURNS + WHIPS SOMEONE ELSE AS SHORT ROUND TURNS TO SEE WHO HIT HIM.

AS THE GUARD MOVES AWAY, SHORT ROUND LIFTS THE ROCK HIGH AND SMASHES....

INTERIOR: THE TEMPLE OF DOOM—
NIGHT

A sea of frightening faces once again intones the horrible sacrificial chant. Among the worshippers is the little maharajah, who sits on a raised platform. Like the other believers, he stares across the crevasse at the altar of Kali Ma.

INTERIOR: THE TEMPLE ALTAR

And once again the three sacred Sankara Stones glow magically. Chattar Lal, dressed in ceremonial robes, stands next to Indiana before the altar. Mola Ram materializes evilly amidst the swirling smoke and begins chanting in Sanskrit. There is a mystical marking on Indy's forehead, and with vacant eyes he stares hypnotically at the High Priest and translates his words.

INDIANA *(translating):* Kali Ma protects us. We are her children. We pledge our devotion to her with an offering of flesh…

Suddenly there is a heart-rending scream of terror and the priests drag forward the next sacrificial victim.

WILLIE *(off screen):* What are you doing?
INDIANA: *(continuing):* …and blood.

Indiana watches without emotion as Willie is brought out. Dressed in a Rajput maiden's outfit, Willie has been jeweled and draped with flowers—a strange contrast as she struggles desperately to escape!

CHATTAR LAL: Your friend has seen and she has heard. Now she will not *talk.*

Once again the iron frame is lowered to the floor, and Willie is dragged toward the sacrificial deep fryer.

WILLIE: I'm not gonna have anything nice to say about this place when I get back. Indy, for God's sake help me! *(cries)* What's the matter with you?!

Chanting in Sanskrit, Mola Ram approaches Willie as two priests force her into the frame. His hand raises menacingly toward her chest, then moves up to stroke her cheek. Abruptly, he turns to Indy, who remains impassive and uncaring as Willie struggles against her restraints.

MOLA RAM *(to Indiana):* Come. Come.
WILLIE *(to Indiana):* Indiana. *(cries)* Indiana. Help us.

Indy looks away from Willie's terrified face and stares up adoringly at the monstrous statue of his goddess Kali.

INTERIOR: THE MINE

In the dark tunnel, a rock smashes down onto a chain—and breaks it! Short Round is exhausted. He looks around furtively and sees a guard approaching.

INTERIOR: THE ALTAR

Indiana walks slowly to Willie and, hypnotically, begins to stroke her face.

CLOSE UP ANGLE ON MOLA RAM - CHANTING.   A BLAST OF RED FIRELIGHT ON CUT.

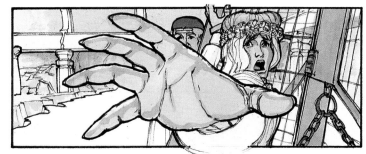

(WILLIE): " INDY ! HELP ME !!! "   DISTORTED HAND (WIDE ANGLE LENS) ALL THE WAY INTO CAM.

OVER INDY TO WILLIE - TENDERLY.

CLOSE UP — WRIST LOCKS CLICK!

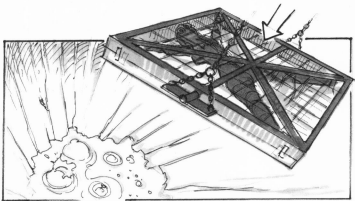

WILLIE: Please snap out of it. You're not one of them. You're not one of them. Please come back to us. Don't leave me.

INTERIOR: THE MINE

His chains broken, Short Round decides to take a chance. He dives and rolls across the tunnel. He ducks behind a mine car full of rocks being pushed out by two children.

The guard lumbers past unsuspectingly as Short Round makes his escape using the moving mine car as cover.

INTERIOR: THE ALTAR

Up in the temple, Willie continues to struggle. Willie's free hand reaches out imploringly toward Indy.

WILLIE: No!

Chanting now in Sanskirt, he reaches out slowly, and Willie grabs his hand tightly. Indy looks into her eyes and then stares at her hand—and slowly lifts it and shackles it to the iron frame.

WILLIE: What are you doing?! Are you mad?!

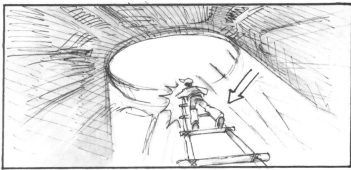

Willie cries in disbelief as Indiana calmly closes the frame, locking her inside.

INTERIOR: THE MINES BELOW

Short Round races up a tunnel and then flattens himself around a corner. He peers anxiously into a large cavern and sees two guards walking away.

INTERIOR: THE ALTAR

In a final act of defiance, Willie spits in Indy's face. His only response is to calmly wipe the spittle from his chin...and smile.

INTERIOR: THE MINES BELOW

When the coast is clear, Short Round darts across the cavern to a long wooden ladder tilted up against the wall. Short Round looks up the high ladder and sees a boy with a sack of rocks descending from a burrow-hole halfway up the wall.

The exhausted kid nearly collapses at the bottom, then jumps, seeing Short Round. Shorty motions for him to keep quiet. Amazed, the boy watches Short Round scramble up the ladder, pursued now by a guard. Shorty continues until he is high above the floor with the shouting guard close behind.

Dirty faces stare out of the high burrow as Short Round stops climbing. The children are astonished as Short Round suddenly grunts and kicks the ladder away from the wall!

The high ladder falls in an arc and what seems like sure suicide slowly resembles a mini–Indiana Jones stunt as Short Round swings to the other side of the falling ladder.

Halfway through the ladder's arc, he grabs a rope hanging from the ceiling. As the children cheer, Short Round scurries up the

*Production stills by
Keith Hamshere
Storyboards by Edward Verreaux*

rope and pulls himself up through an opening in the ceiling and into the chamber behind the altar.

INTERIOR: THE TEMPLE OF DOOM

Chains clink and gears grind as the sacrificial frame and victim are turned face-down and the heavy stone doors slowly open to reveal the molten death at the bottom of the chasm.

WILLIE: This can't be happening. This can't be happening. *(off-screen)* Wake up, Willie, wake up.

Production stills by Keith Hamshere

As one of the demonic priests pushes the lever, Willie begins to descend slowly into the crevasse while the crowd chants louder. She screams in terror.

WILLIE: No! No!

INTERIOR: THE REAR CHAMBER

Short Round dashes across the dark chamber behind the altar. He peers out and sees Willie disappearing into the crevasse as Indiana watches impassively. Shorty races to Indy's side and grabs his hand imploringly.

SHORT ROUND: Wake up, Dr. Jones! Wake up!

Indy jerks his hand from Short Round's grasp, swings, and back-hands the little guy across the face, knocking him to the floor.

Storyboard by Edward Verreaux
Below: The mechanical puppet
of Kate Capshaw used for miniature effects shots; for example,
the lava pit shot. Photo by
Kerry Nordquist

Short Round, with tears in this eyes, stares at his hero in
wounded disbelief.

SHORT ROUND: Doctor Jones!

Recovering quickly, Short Round springs to his feet and runs, pursued once again by guards. He grabs for a wall torch and just
manages to yank it free. Using the torch to keep the guards at
bay, Shorty scrambles back to Indiana.

SHORT ROUND: Indy, I love you!

Short Round lunges at Indiana and jams the torch into his side.
The fiery torch burns Indy, smoking as it sears his flesh, and he
yells in pain.

SHORT ROUND: Wake up! Wake up!

As Indy crumples to the ground, a temple guard rushes to Short
Round and grabs the torch from him. Another guard moves forward and pulls a knife from his belt.

SHORT ROUND (to Indiana): You're my best friend! Wake up,
Indy!

Rising slowly from the floor, Indiana shakes his head as if awak-
ening from a dream and turns to the guards who are holding
Short Round.

INDIANA: Wait! Wait! He's mine.

Short Round is frightened as Indy grabs him from the guards. He
lifts Short Round into the air and holds him on the crevasse, an
inch from doom. Shorty is terrified...until Indiana flashes him a
quick smile and winks!

INDIANA: I'm all right, kid.

Then Indiana sets Short Round down safely, whirls, and punches
the guard in the face! Short Round also springs into action, stop-
ping another guard with a quick karate kick in the stomach.

*Production stills by
Keith Hamshere
Storyboards by Andrew G. Probert*

*Opposite page: Production still by
Keith Hamshere; Storyboards by
Andrew G. Probert*

*Another guard works the control lever, lowering the sacrificial
frame. Down in the crevasse, Willie screams as the iron frame
suddenly plummets toward the fulminating lava!*

*On the platform, Indiana dives for the lever and manages to stop
it.*

*Down in the crevasse, the frame jolts to a stop only yards above
the spumes of fiery lava. The heat is so intense now that Willie's
clothes start smoking and she passes out.*

INTERIOR: THE TEMPLE

*The chanting stops as the Kali worshippers notice the battle on
the altar. The little maharajah looks concerned, and his guards
move him out through the crowd.*

INTERIOR: THE ALTAR

*Mola Ram removes his headdress as Indiana runs toward him,
holding a spear.*

INDIANA: Mola Ram!

*With a triumphant laugh, Mola Rum lies down on the floor in
front of the statue of Kali, and suddenly disappears as he triggers
a secret trapdoor.*

*Seeing his quarry vanish, Indiana throws aside the spear and
turns to the wheel. He cranks furiously. The frame holding Willie
begins to rise.*

*As the frame appears above the opening, Chattar Lal leaps onto
the crankwheel platform and Indy sees him pull a dagger. He
slashes at Indiana as he releases the control lever—the gears
scream and the chains screech! The iron frame plunges again
toward the crimson lava!*

*On the platform, Indy hears the frame lowering and looks pan-
icked. Chattar Lal slashes again with the dagger, keeping Indy
away from the cogwheel mechanism.*

*Indy suddenly kicks the dagger from Chattar Lal's hand, slugs
him, and knocks him back over the cogwheel mechanism. The
gears slam to a stop with Chattar Lal pinned underneath. Indiana grabs the crankwheel and starts winding it up furiously.
Short Round runs to help Indiana turn the wheel, and the sacrificial frame rises up into view. Indiana grabs it and swings it over
toward the platform, yelling to Short Round.*

INDIANA: Gimme some slack!

He looks at Willie anxiously as he releases her bindings.

INDIANA: Willie! Willie! Wake up!

CHATTER L'AL - EYES GLOWING, FULLY TRANSFORMED - CHARGES THE CAMERA....

.... INTO A TERRIFYING CLOSE UP !

INTERIOR: THE MINES

The slave children are working in the tunnels, dragging carts filled with rocks they have chopped out of the caverns. One girl falls, others urge her to get up as a guard stands over the girl with a whip.

Indiana stands in silhouette, watching the scene before him. Suddenly, he flattens the guard with a mighty punch.

INTERIOR: THE TUNNEL

Willie flattens against the wall as Indiana catapults the guard past her back into the mine, where he's set upon by a horde of rebellious slave children.

The kids swarm over the guard like jackals, and we see Willie pull a key from the fallen guard's robe.

Willie moans and moves her head. Indiana pulls her off the frame and she starts coughing. Gasping for breath, Willie revives as fresh air flows into her lungs. She opens her eyes and sees Indiana, and slaps him in the face.

INDIANA: Willie! Willie, it's me! I'm back.
WILLIE: Oh, Indy.

They kiss as Short Round runs up and tosses Indiana's satchel to him. Indy quickly stuffs the glowing Sankara Stones into the bag, then, gently, puts Shorty's New York Yankees cap on the boy's head. Short Round hands Indiana's battered felt hat to him. A hero should never be without his hat. Indiana kneels down and hugs Short Round.

SHORT ROUND: Indy, my friend.
INDIANA: I'm sorry, kid.
WILLIE: Indy, now let's get outta here.
INDIANA: Right! *All* of us.

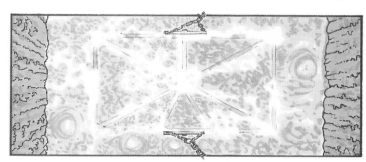

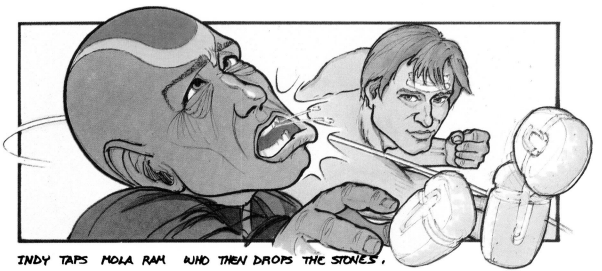
INDY TAPS MOLA RAM WHO THEN DROPS THE STONES.

MONTAGE: THE MINES

A key is twisted and the chains are pulled from kids' legs…

Elsewhere, more chains are unlocked and rattle free. Liberated kids spill out of the tunnels…

A guard is tripped and attacked by a horde of ex-slaves…

High up on a ledge, kids pour baskets of rocks down to disable more guards…

EXTERIOR/INTERIOR: PANKOT PALACE—DAY

Freed children swarm through the Pleasure Pavilion, running over the banquet table and cushions, racing joyously out of the palace into the sunshine.

INTERIOR: THE MINES

… CONTINUES TO MOVE IN AND AROUND TO THE RIGHT. INDY SEES A CAR BEING DUMPED AND THEN SHOVED DOWN A TRACK.
(INDY): "THOSE EMPTY CARS HAVE TO GO OUT OF THE MINES."

*Production stills by
Keith Hamshere
Storyboard by Andrew G. Probert*

Indiana turns—and looks into the bare chest of the giant Thuggee guard. Indy has to look up to see the man's mean-looking face.

Indiana grabs a sledgehammer and hits the giant in the stomach. The giant does not even flinch, he just grabs the hammer and flings it away. It clangs down on another guard's head, knocking him out.

Short Round starts toward the fighters but Willie grabs him, holding him tightly as the guard slams Indiana against a mine car, then doubles him over with a punch in the stomach.

WILLIE: No!
SHORT ROUND: I gotta save him!
WILLIE: He can take care of himself.
SHORT ROUND: He needs me. I gotta save Indy!

Short Round struggles. Indiana groans as the Thuggee picks him up bodily and carries him toward an empty mine car.

WILLIE: Okay, save him.

Short Round picks up a whip and follows the enormous guard carrying Indy, hitting the man's legs futilely. The giant only laughs.

SHORT ROUND: Drop him down! I kill you! Drop him down!

The guard drops Indiana into the cart, then picks up the yelling Short Round and throws him aside.

The car is being dragged up the dump ramp and the giant jumps into it after Indiana. As the giant rushes him, Indy kicks him, then smashes his fist against the big man's face, without any effect at all.

Suddenly Indy yells as he feels a stabbing pain in his back.

CAR NEARS THE TOP OF THE INCLINE — THE GUARD GOES FOR INDY.

INDY SCREAMS, COLLAPSES, AND GRABS HIS LEG.

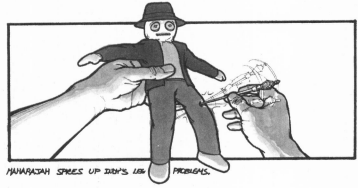

MAHARAJAH SPICES UP INDY'S LEG PROBLEMS.

WILLIE: What's the matter with him?

Shorty is confused and worried—and then he sees something! He looks up, and there, on a rock-cut balcony over the cavern, is the little maharajah!

The little prince clutches the clay krtya *doll that represents Indy. He jabs it in the back with a long sapphire-tipped turban pin.*

On the mine car, Indy yells again and falls backward as the car dumps him and the giant onto the moving conveyor belt. Short Round takes off. He dashes under the platform toward a bucket-chain carrying spent water back up to the cistern.

Short Round leaps over the pool of water and grabs onto a bucket. He rises up on this makeshift elevator toward the rock balcony and the malicious little maharajah.

Meanwhile, Indy is on the brink of unconsciousness as the giant's massive hands throttle his neck.

Down below, Willie hands a metal can up to Indiana, who clobbers the guard and gets the advantage for the moment.

WILLIE: Here, try this.

Near the waterfall, Short Round ascends on the rising bucket-chain. Up on the balcony, the little maharajah chuckles evilly as he watches Indiana on the conveyor belt.

The maharajah lifts the clay doll and viciously jabs the pin into the back of it!

On the conveyor, Indiana yells as the stabbing pain lacerates his back! He falls and writhes helplessly as the giant staggers up the rocky conveyor belt toward him.

Willie sees Indy's desperate situation as he's pulled along the conveyor toward the rock-crusher! She looks up and sees Short Round leap from the bucket-chain onto the balcony. The little maharajah's eyes gleam maliciously as he lifts the clay doll—and jabs the pin again.

On the conveyor belt, Indy yells agonizingly. Behind him, rocks explode as they're crushed and pulverized by the mammoth roller.

Short Round dashes across the balcony and tackles the maharajah. They fall and fight like mortal enemies. The krtya *doll, with the pin stuck through it, falls to the ground, just out of reach of Short Round's desperately searching hand.*

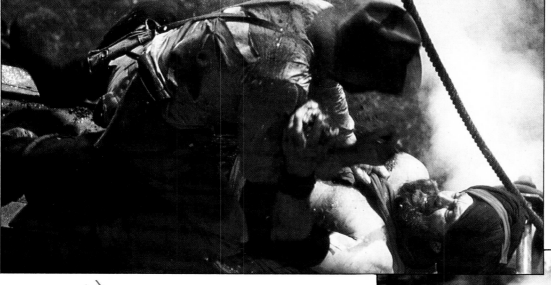

Opposite page: (left) Storyboards by Andrew G. Probert; (middle right) Storyboard by Edward Verreaux; (bottom) Production still by Keith Hamshere

Production stills by Keith Hamshere
Storyboards by Edward Verreaux

Only a few feet away from the rock-smashing roller, Indy is still on his back on the conveyor belt, thrashing in pain, feeling the maharajah's pin piercing his back.

On the balcony, Short Round punches the maharajah in the face and dives for the clay doll. He pulls out the pin!

On the conveyor belt, Indiana is suddenly released from the pain, grabs a saw, and hits the giant in the stomach. They trade punches, being pulled closer and closer to the rock crusher. The giant picks up a huge rock and miscalculates his timing—he drops it on his own head.

The sash around his waist is caught under the rolling crusher and he's dragged back under it feet first. The Thuggee giant screams hideously as his body is rolled over and squashed by the enormous stone wheel.

On the balcony, Short Round is rolling around, trading punches with the little maharajah. He grabs a torch from a wall sconce, and, as the prince attacks with a knife, jabs the torch against his hand. The maharajah looks like he's just awakened from a bad dream.

SHORT ROUND: It was the black sleep of Kali.

Meanwhile, Indy runs along the catwalk above the conveyor belt.

Opposite page: Stop Motion Animator Tom St. Amand changes puppet positions for a mine tunnel shot. Photo by Kerry Nordquist; Mine tunnel set blueprint by Stephen Scott

Production stills by Keith Hamshere Storyboard by Edward Verreaux Below: Effects Cameraman Rick Fichter checks a camera angle on the lava tunnel set. Photo by Kerry Nordquist

He jumps and grabs onto a cross-bar. He kicks out with his feet and knocks a quarry guard off the catwalk. The guard flies through the air and topples into the sand pit, where he thrashes around blindly under the sand falling from the crusher.

Across the cavern, Willie shoves a rolling mine car toward the balcony.

INDIANA: Short Round! Quit foolin' around with that kid. Get down on the floor, now.
SHORT ROUND: Okey, dokey, Indy.

Up on the rock balcony, Short Round lowers himself over the edge. The little maharajah grabs his arm.

MAHARAJAH: Please, listen. To get out you must take the left tunnel.

Shorty looks at him and he knows he's telling the truth.

SHORT ROUND: Thank you.

Short Round slips over the edge and slides down to the floor of the cavern.

There he finds Willie pushing an empty mine car, trying to get it rolling. Short Round fights his way toward her, kicking and hitting the guards as Willie jumps into the now-moving car.

Across the quarry, Mola Ram and six temple guards run out onto a high platform next to the waterfall.

Mola Ram shouts to his men—Two of them pull pistols and open fire!

Meanwhile, up on a catwalk, a guard slices a sword through the air and Indiana ducks! The sword slashes into a wooden railing and the guard tries frantically to pull it out.

Indiana slams his knee up into the guard's stomach and then smashes his fist down on his neck; the man collapses. Indy hears more gunfire.

INDIANA: Shorty! Quit stallin'! Go! Go!

Short Round runs toward the cart holding Willie, which is starting to roll. He falls down under a guard clinging to the cart.

WILLIE: Shorty, look out!

The clinging guard is pulled along, making a human ramp, and Short Round runs right up his body and jumps into the cart.

Indiana spots the rolling mine car racing across the quarry. He takes off and runs along the catwalk. Bullets explode around him, splintering wood. Indy reaches the end of the catwalk—

Suddenly he dives into the air and catches hold of a block and tackle! Indy skids along the pulley system, sliding down a cable toward the mine car in which Short Round and Willie are riding.

SHORT ROUND: Come on, Indy.
WILLIE: Hurry!
SHORT ROUND: Hurry! Hurry up!

Bullets whiz past as Indiana sails in the air above the speeding mine car. When they are in sync, Indy lets go and drops into the

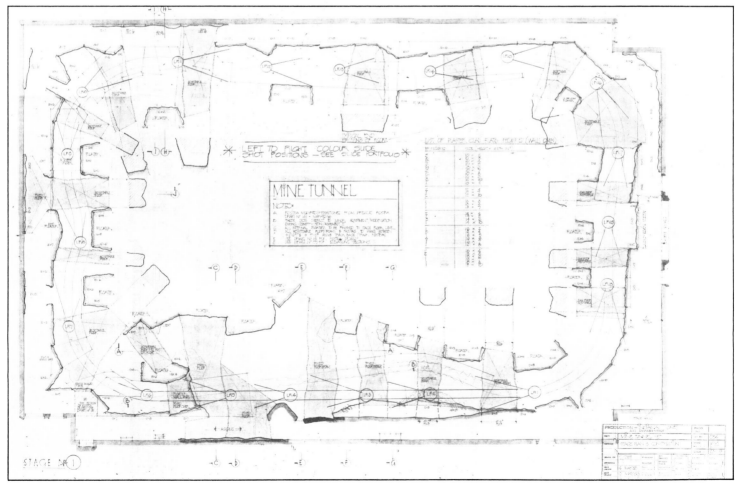

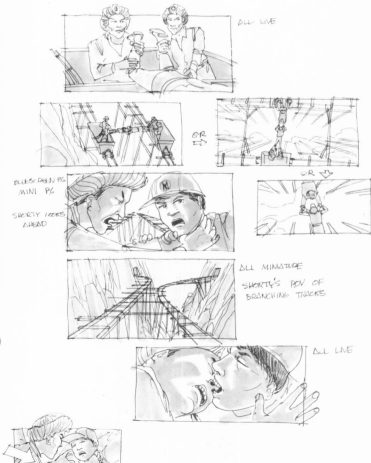

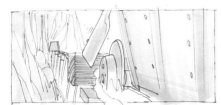

C.U. RIFLE BUTT PUSHING BEAM...
BEAM WON'T BUDGE

BLUESCREEN P.G. OR
ALL LIVE

ALL MINIATURE

CONTINUED

ALL LIVE
BAD GUYS PEEKS OVER EDGE
OF MINE CAR.

*Production stills by
Keith Hamshere
Sketches and storyboards by
Joe Johnston
Above: Assistant Cameraman Joe
Fulmer adjusts the set for a mine
car over lava shot. Photo by
Kerry Nordquist*

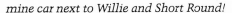

mine car next to Willie and Short Round!

Mola Ram rushes forward and watches the speeding mine car rolling down the track toward the tunnels. He shouts orders to his guards.

In the speeding mine car, Indy sees the tracks separating in two directions—one back into the quarry, the other toward two tunnels that lead out of the mines.

Indiana lifts a shovel from the floor of the car and swings it just in time. He hits a switch, which CLANGS as they speed by, and the car is shunted tipsy-turvy onto the track toward the two tunnels.

Willie hangs on as the car tears down the track toward the tunnel on the right...and Short Round looks worried.

SHORT ROUND: Indy, it's the left tunnel! The left tunnel. It should be that—the *left* tunnel!

But it's too late and they all hold on as the mine car shoots down into the darkness of the echoing tunnel.

INTERIOR: THE TUNNEL

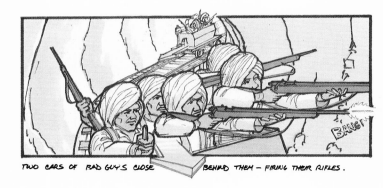

TWO CARS OF BAD GUYS CLOSE   BEHIND THEM - FIRING THEIR RIFLES.

The wind rushes past Indiana as the car descends into the tunnel and picks up speed. Willie hangs on with Short Round. The mine car roars around a curve and flies faster along the rails.

INTERIOR: THE QUARRY

Back in the quarry, Mola Ram supervises his guards as they shove empty cars toward the tunnel. Carrying long Khyber rifles, they jump aboard the cars. The first one rolls into the dark tunnel, and the second car speeds after it.

INTERIOR: THE TUNNEL ENTRANCE

The two Thuggee cars shoot past, descending into the darkness in pursuit of the infidels who have stolen the Sankara Stones.

INTERIOR: THE TUNNEL

The mine car hurtles past. Indy sits in front, pulling back on the brake lever to control their speed and keep them from careening off the tracks.

Expecting trouble, Short Round peers over the back end of the car. Willie ducks low, watching the heavy beams flashing dangerously close over their heads.

Then Willie's eyes go wide and she groans in terror like a girl on a roller coaster as the mine car suddenly plunges downward, taking their stomachs with it.

A gunshot rings out and Short Round sees the first Thuggee car appear around a curve behind them. Mola Ram's gunmen start blasting. Bullets ricochet off the mine car and Indy yells back to Short Round.

INDIANA: We got company.

Short Round scurries forward and grabs the brake from Indy.

HE SPINS AROUND AND SHOUTS (STOP LOADING) TO HIS MEN — AND THEN POINTS TO THE CISTERN.

Opposite page: Storyboard by Andrew G. Probert; sketch by Stanley Fleming

Left: storyboard by Andrew G. Probert Below: storyboards by Edward Verreaux

INDIANA *(continuing):* Let her go. Let go of the brake.
SHORT ROUND: What?
INDIANA: Let her go! It's our only chance to outrun 'em!

Short Round looks scared as Indy releases the brake and the car hurtles toward a curve. They grab the sides of the car as it tips precariously. Behind them, the curve throws the gunmen from side to side in the car following.

Willie closes her eyes as they rocket toward the curve. In the car behind, the Thuggee guard at the brake also shoves the brake off—and looks extremely worried.

Indy's car hits the curve, and the centrifugal force lifts the inside wheels off the rails!

Willie and Short Round jump over to his side as the car whips around the curve! Indy looks back and sees the car pursuing them is also taking the curve at full speed.

INDIANA: Shorty!
SHORT ROUND: Huh?
INDIANA: Come up here and take the brake. Watch it on the curves or we'll fly right off the track.
SHORT ROUND: Okay!

INTERIOR: THE TUNNEL

Indiana hefts a railroad tie out of the bottom of the car and Willie watches him lift it onto the back.

As gunfire continues to explode from the car behind them, Indiana shoves the railroad tie off the back of the car.

The wooden tie falls and bounces back across the tracks. The gunmen in the car behind spot it and yell in panic.

Indy and Willie watch the gunmen's car crash into the railroad tie. The guards scream horribly as the car tumbles end over end, slamming against the tunnel walls, getting ripped to shreds so that finally only pieces of metal, wheels, and debris fly like a meteorite shower down the tunnel!

The two cars run on parallel tracks above a river of molten lava. Short Round, screaming in terror, is stretched between the cars. They race toward a rock divider, and just in time Indiana pulls Shorty back into their car.

Now the guards' car runs above them and Willie screams as one of the Thuggees leaps down on them, grappling with Indiana. They struggle desperately and the guard goes down, but as Indy turns, the guard suddenly reappears behind him. Willie punches him one in the face and the guard falls in front of the Thuggee mine car. The car hits him and goes over the edge.

Indiana turns around and suddenly they all see, ahead of them, that the track ends! Indy pushes Willie and Short Round down and the mine car flies off the end of the track, sails through empty space, then lands with a thump on the far side and continues down the track.

INTERIOR: THE CAVERN

Willie and Short Round whoop for joy. They hear more gunshots, and a second mine car full of guards appears behind them.

INTERIOR: THE CAVERN

Up in the quarry, Mola Ram shouts orders to his men, who take sledgehammers and begin to bash away at the supports under the huge water-filled cistern. Water laps dangerously over the edge as the huge tank creaks and sways.

INTERIOR: THE TUNNEL

The walls of the tunnel flash past and curves appear out of the darkness as the hair-raising chase continues. Indiana stands, holding the shovel.

WILLIE: What are you doing?
INDIANA: Short cut!
SHORT ROUND: …What, Indy?
INDIANA: Short *cut!*

Indiana hits a lever with the shovel and the car swerves onto a new track and crashes through a sign marked DANGER. By shooting at the switch, the pursuing guards shunt their car onto a different track and they run up parallel. Indiana grabs a rifle as the guards run side by side with them. A guard reaches out and grabs Short Round by the arms. Indy holds tightly onto Short Round's legs, trying to pull him back.

INDIANA: Watch it!
SHORT ROUND: Indy, help! Oh, Indy!
WILLIE: Pull him in!

Opposite page: Model maker Paul Huston works on the miniature cistern set. Photo by Terry Chostner; storyboards by Edward Verreaux

Production stills by Keith Hamshere Storyboard by Edward Verreaux

The sledgehammers continue, until two of the supports give way. There are shouts as the guards run for cover.

Mola Ram stands on a platform watching the huge cistern slowly keel over. The noise is incredible as the colossal tank crashes to the ground!

Suddenly a half million gallons of water explode across the cavern and surge in a tidal wave toward the tunnels.

INTERIOR: THE TUNNEL

The guards disposed of, the mine car continues its mad course through the tunnels.

INDIANA: All right.
WILLIE: What?
INDIANA: Brake. Brake. Slow us down!
SHORT ROUND: Okay.

Short Round dives for the front of the car and happily pulls the brake lever—it doesn't work! Short Round yanks on it harder. The brake lever suddenly breaks off!

SHORT ROUND: Uh-oh. Big mistake! Big mistake, Indy.
WILLIE: Figures.

Indy sees Short Round holding up the broken brake lever! Indy crawls quickly toward Shorty, while Willie holds on for dear life!

Completely out of control, the car hurtles down a decline into a section where the tunnel is larger again.

Indiana bends over the front of the car, looks underneath, and sees the brake tension hanging loose from the brake pad. He slips

*Storyboards by Edward Verreaux
Sketch by Joe Johnston*

over the front of the car and swings a leg underneath.

Indy is inches above the rails with the rocky ground blurring beneath the car as he tries to kick at the brake pad. His feet fall and he bumps along, dragged dangerously for a moment.

Indy manages to find a foothold on the undercarriage of the car. He kicks again and his foot hits the brake pad. He shoves it, and slowly the pad closes against the spinning wheel…

WILLIE: We're going too fast!
SHORT ROUND: Help!

Willie and Short Round look up and see that the tunnel is ending ahead and the track dead-ends into a stone wall!

WILLIE: Too fast! We're gonna crash!

Indy's foot is kicking in high gear underneath the car. He slams at the brake pad with all his strength. The pad screeches against the spinning wheel, starts sparking and breaks off!

The car seems to slow as it shoots toward the end of the tunnel. Indy groans and pushes harder against the wheel itself, as smoke starts to billow.

The car slows more and more until it runs down the last few yards to the dead end and rolls gently to a stop, just nudging Indy's back against the wall.

Indiana breathes heavily, and laughs in sheer relief. Then he feels something and looks down: his shoe is smoking! He jumps around stomping on the ground and moaning.

INDIANA: Water! Water! Water!
WILLIE: Oh, look!
INDIANA: Water! Water!
WILLIE: Oh, you're on fire!

Indy continues his frantic, foot-stomping jig as Willie kicks dirt on his smoldering shoe.

A rumbling behind them sounds increasingly ominous. Indiana looks up and stops dead in his tracks—paralyzed—awestruck—DOOMED!

INDIANA: Water!

He sees a monster wall of water (released from the quarry) as it thunders around a curve, a mammoth tidal wave crashing spectacularly against the opposite tunnel wall!

A veritable tsunami is caroming off the tunnel wall and spewing furiously forward like a hydrous Juggernaut!

INDIANA *(continuing):* Come on! Come on!

All three of them take off, running faster than they've ever run in their lives!

The tidal wave smashes forward, booming behind them, and Indiana realizes quickly that they're going to lose this race. Suddenly he sees a small side tunnel ahead.

*Above, left: The ILM miniature water tunnel set. Photo by Kerry Nordquist
Production stills by Keith Hamshere*

Opposite page: (top) Matte artist Caroleen Green puts the finishing touches on a cliff face matte painting. Photo by Kerry Nordquist. (bottom) The Empire High Speed camera captures the falling water. In slow motion, the water will appear to be the proper scale. Photo by Terry Chostner

Matte painting by Chris Evans Near right: Frame enlargement

They lunge toward the hole, and Short Round dives in it first. Indiana shoves Willie into the hole and jumps in after her—just as the colossal tidal wave explodes past!

INTERIOR: THE SMALL TUNNEL

They are in a small side tunnel, apparently at an angle to the main path of the rushing current, which passes by them. The roar of the tidal wave recedes a bit as they catch their breath.

Suddenly an EXPLOSION! They turn and see the thundering tidal wave crashing around a curve and cascading down the tunnel behind them again!

SHORT ROUND: Let's go!

They all holler in unison and start running like bats out of hell toward the daylight. The towering wall of water surges relentlessly after them.

The tidal wave looms up to annihilate them as they race to the mouth of the tunnel—as they exit into the sunlight, Willie SCREAMS! Indy grabs her and all three of them flail their arms to keep from losing their balance!

EXTERIOR: THE TUNNEL EXIT—DAY

The tunnel exits midway up a cliff and the three totter precariously on the brink looking down at a 300-foot sheer drop to a gorge below!

Indiana swings Willie onto a narrow ledge on one side and pushes Short Round after her. He jumps himself to the other side—just as the tidal wave crashes past them!

The water bursts out of the tunnel. The gusher spews forth water and debris from the cliffside into the air as if Hoover Dam just broke loose!

103

Opposite page: Storyboard by
Andrew G. Probert; Production
still by Eva Sereny

Storyboard by Andrew G. Probert
Below: Matte artists Caroleen
Green and Frank Ordaz paint a
backdrop painting for the cliff
face water tunnel shot. Photo by
Terry Chostner

Short Round and Willie balance on the narrow ledge on one side
of the geyser. Indy is perched on the ledge on the other side of the
incredible eruption of water.

The pressure of the water slams a log out through the cliff face
near Indiana's head. Willie screams as another log slams through
above her.

SHORT ROUND: Willie, look out!

The ledge beneath her feet crumbles away and she moves off to
the side seeking solid footing. Indiana falls forward grabbing a
new hold as the log he's clinging to is washed away.

Willie gets vertigo looking down into the gorge where the water
crashes at the bottom.

There is a rope bridge swinging about twenty feet above Willie
and Short Round. Indy shouts across the blasting water.

INDIANA: Head for the bridge!

Willie looks frightened.

SHORT ROUND: Come on, Willie. This way.

He edges along the narrow ledge toward the bridge, and Willie
follows him.

Meanwhile, Indiana is scaling the cliff face to get over the water
geyser to the other side. He grabs at scrub brush and finds a few
perilous footholds as he makes his way to the bridge.

EXTERIOR: THE ROPE BRIDGE

Willie and Short Round pull themselves up at the end of the
bridge. What's in front of them is hardly reassuring.

The rope bridge across the gorge is a century old and definitely
wasn't built by army engineers. Lying across the two bottom rope
spans, worm-eaten and moldy boards offer risky footings.

Vertical side ropes connect the bottom rope spans to the two
upper ropes that constitute the dangerous hand railings.

WILLIE: Oh, God.
SHORT ROUND: Come on. Let's go.

Short Round steps tentatively out onto the bridge. It holds him
and he turns and smiles at Willie.

SHORT ROUND: Strong bridge. Come on, let's go. Strong bridge!

He jumps up and down to prove his point.

SHORT ROUND: Look, strong wood! Come on!

Suddenly the board under him breaks. With a wail he falls
through the bridge, catching on desperately with his hands.

SHORT ROUND: I'm falling down!
WILLIE: Shorty!
SHORT ROUND: Help! I'm falling down! Help!

In the water below hungry crocodiles thrash as Short Round dan-
gles helplessly above them. Willie crawls toward the boy and
hauls him up through the broken slats.

SHORT ROUND: Not very funny.

Short Round starts out again, and Willie follows him carefully.

They continue stepping across the bridge cautiously, a feat made
more difficult by the bridge's constant swaying and heart-stop-
ping up-and-down movement.

Behind them, Indy heads toward the bridge. He hears something and turns quickly as two Thuggee guards rush out, swinging their swords in an elaborate attack pattern.

Indiana reaches for his side holster, opens the flap, and finds—no gun! He hits the first guard and ducks under his sword arm, grabbing him from behind and using the guard's sword arm to engage in a duel with the second guard.

He shoves both guards out of the way, frees his whip, and cracks it around a guard's wrist, pulling the sword from his hand. Indy looks at the unfamiliar weapon, hefts it, and tries to decide quickly the best way to use it.

He decides that shouting must be the de rigueur technique, shouts loudly, and charges after the guard with whip and sword. The charge brings him face to face with a larger group of guards, and he reverses direction immediately.

Keeping the sword, Indy starts out onto the bridge, walking as quickly as possible across the rickety span. He hears shouting ahead and looks worried when temple guards appear at the far end of the bridge.

Mola Ram and his guards surprise Willie and Shorty as they finally get across the bridge, and quickly take them prisoner.

MOLA RAM: Welcome.

Indy stands helpless in the middle of the swaying bridge with Mola Ram in front of him and nothing but heaven above and the rocky river gorge filled with crocodiles hundreds of feet below!

The wind whips around Indy and he staggers unsteadily on the swaying bridge as he watches Mola Ram.

INDIANA: Let her go, Mola Ram.
MOLA RAM: You are in a position unsuitable to give orders.
WILLIE *(to Indiana):* Watch your back!

Indiana turns and sees more of the temple guards starting across the bridge behind him. He pulls off the bag over his shoulder and holds it out dangling over the bridge.

INDIANA: You want the stones? Let 'em go! Let her go!
MOLA RAM *(laughs):* Drop them, Dr. Jones. They will be found. You won't.
SHORT ROUND: Indy!

A CROCODILE EXPLODES FROM UNDER WATER ATTACKING THE BOARDS

INDY — TRAPPED

Production stills by
Keith Hamshere
Top two storyboards by
Andrew G. Probert
Bottom storyboard by
Edward Verreaux

*Production stills by
Keith Hamshere*

WILLIE: Behind you!

Mola Ram shouts in Hindi and the guards both before and behind him move closer. Indiana secures the bag with the stones around his neck and considers his situation. The guards move closer and draw their swords.

INDIANA: Oh, shit!

He lifts the sword and tests it against the rope side, then raises it above his head.

Mola Ram, looking more nervous now, gestures with his knife toward Willie and Short Round, motioning them toward the bridge.

MOLA RAM: Go on! Go!

Willie gasps and reluctantly begins to walk out onto the bridge.

Opposite page: (top) Frame enlargement; (bottom) Unit at work on the cliff face set at EMI-Elstree Studios. Photos by Keith Hamshere

Storyboards by Edward Verreaux Production stills by Keith Hamshere

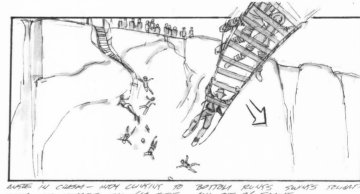

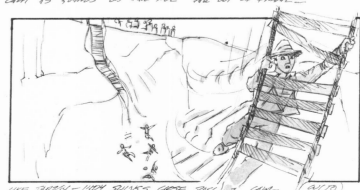

MOLA RAM: Go on, go on. Get going!

Still holding the sword poised above his head, Indiana carefully hooks his leg around the webbing of the side spans.

INDIANA: Shorty!

Indiana speaks rapidly to Short Round in Chinese. The boy nods, then twists a rope span securely around his arm.

SHORT ROUND: Hang on, lady. We goin' for a ride!
WILLIE: Oh, my God. Oh, my God. Oh, my God.

Petrified, she also wraps the rope around her wrist. Indiana raises the sword higher.

WILLIE: Oh my god. Is he nuts?
SHORT ROUND: He no nuts. He crazy.
INDIANA: Mola Ram, prepare to meet Kali…in hell!
MOLA RAM: What are you doing?!

Indiana swings the sword and cuts into one of the top rope spans. The rope is half severed and frays slowly under the tension.

Indiana swings the sword with all his might. It whooshes through the air and slashes clear through the top and bottom ropes!

Immediately Mola Ram's guards start to flee in panic—too late! The rope bridge is sheared in two! It breaks in the middle, and both halves fall apart! The guards scream horribly in the air as they plunge down into the rocky gorge!

Willie and Short Round cling to their established footholds and fall with the bridge toward the wall of the gorge. Mola Ram spills forward, clutching desperately at ropes and slats.

Below them, Indiana has latched onto a rope and swings with the bridge as it hits the gorge wall and hangs vertically now, dangling from its moorings at the top.

There's an instant of suspended animation as all who remain alive realize they are alive. Short Round and Willie cling near the top of the now vertical bridge.

Above them, Mola Ram clutches onto one of the main ropes while, directly above him, one of his guards holds on for dear life. Mola Ram climbs upward, and a slat breaks under his hand, sending him plunging down past Short Round and Willie.

MOLA RAM: No!

He catches himself, knocking another of his guards down into the gorge. The crocodiles below are churning and thrashing in the water, feeding on the fallen guards.

Opposite page: (top left) Steven Spielberg rough sketch for Special Effects artist Stan Fleming. Storyboards by Edward Verreaux; Production still by Keith Hamshere

This page: Production stills by Keith Hamshere; Storyboards by Edward Verreaux
Top, left: Director Steven Spielberg with Amrish Puri and Harrison Ford. Photo by Keith Hamshere

Mola Ram's fingers are inching toward Indy's body. Indy clutches at Mola Ram's wrist, trying to keep the deadly fingers away from his heart.

Willie and Short Round watch, horrified, from the ladder above them. Mola Ram laughs and begins chanting in Hindi as his hand moves on Indy's chest.

WILLIE: Oh, my God! Oh, my God.

Slowly Indy is able to push Mola Ram's hand away. His fingers withdraw, but Mola Ram hits him a powerful blow in the face and Indiana falls backward, catching onto the bridge farther down. He clutches his chest with relief as Mola Ram begins to climb up. He grabs his own remaining Thuggee guard around the neck and hurls him downward like a weapon, trying to dislodge Indiana. Indiana dodges sideways, dangling dangerously near the bottom of the bridge.

Across the gorge, the Thuggee guards run up a path to the edge of the plateau above the gorge. The guards have bows and arrows and take firing positions.

SHORT ROUND: Look out!
WILLIE: Nooooo!

Meanwhile, dangling below on the bridge, Indy reaches up and grabs Mola Ram's leg. The High Priest kicks and tries to break Indy's grip. He kicks again, and smashes Indy in the face.

Indy won't let go. He grabs at the back of Mola Ram's robe and pulls him down. Struggling, Mola Ram turns, and it's Indy's chance to punch Mola Ram in the face. Mola Ram's hand thrusts toward Indiana's chest, and Short Round yells from above.

SHORT ROUND: Indy, cover your heart! Cover your heart!

Indy looks down and writhes, terrified, as he sees Mola Ram's hand trying to enter his chest as it entered the victim's chest during the temple sacrifice.

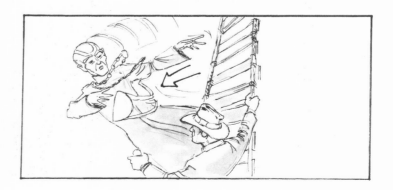

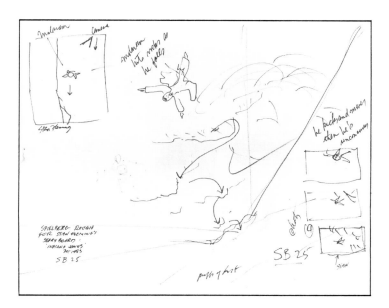

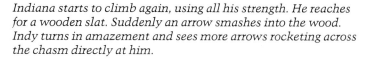

Indiana starts to climb again, using all his strength. He reaches for a wooden slat. Suddenly an arrow smashes into the wood. Indy turns in amazement and sees more arrows rocketing across the chasm directly at him.

INDIANA: Jesus!

Above Indiana on the bridge, Mola Ram keeps climbing until Willie and Short Round start pounding him from above, kicking at his head and hands, trying to throw him off. Mola Ram yells in pain, and slips down, grabbing onto Indiana as he falls past him. The two men almost fall together.

WILLIE: No!
SHORT ROUND: Come on, let's go.

They begin to climb up toward the top of the ladder. Below them, Indiana has managed to keep his hold on the bridge and he struggles desperately with Mola Ram, who has grabbed hold of the bag containing the Sankara Stones.

MOLA RAM: The stones are mine!
INDIANA: You betrayed Shiva. *(He repeats in Sanskrit Sankara's warning.)*

As Indy pronounces the magical words, the bag begins glowing and starts to burn Mola Ram as he clutches it. The stones begin to spill out of the bag, and the High Priest grabs for them.

INDIANA *(continuing): (He repeats Sankara's warning in Sanskrit.)*

The blazing stones sear Mola Ram's flesh and he screams in pain. The light suddenly dies in his eyes, and for one instant he looks at Indy as if awakened from a nightmare.

Mola Ram loses his balance and Indy grabs for the stones. Two fall into the river. He manages to catch the remaining stone as Mola Ram screams and falls!

111

*Opposite page: Production still by
Keith Hamshere*

*Above: Matte painting by
Michael Pangrazio
Near right: Frame enlargement*

then holds up his right hand—and sets the one remaining Sankara Stone on the ground.

EXTERIOR: THE MAYAPORE HILLS—DAY

Brilliant sunshine highlights the rebirth of the once desolate landscape. The village, prosperous again, is in the distance. Streams flow beneath green trees, flowers bloom, and peasants harvest golden grain in the fields.

Indiana, Willie, and Short Round come over a hill and down the dirt road into Mayapore. The villagers come forward to greet them.

Indy sees the stone in his hand suddenly cool. He watches Mola Ram plummeting downward into the chasm and finally crashing into the jagged rocks at the bottom.

The irritated crocodiles are disturbed once more, but soon welcome the meal that just dropped in. Jaws flash and teeth rip at the High Priest's lifeless corpse.

And the two remaining Sankara stones sink into the murky current and disappear down the river…

EXTERIOR: THE CLIFF

At the top of the cliff, the little maharajah appears, pointing toward the Thuggee guards firing arrows across the gorge. He is followed by Captain Blumburtt and his British troops.

WILLIE: Well, it's about time.

The British take aim, and soon the guards across the way give up and run into the woods.

There is no sign of Indiana. Willie and Short Round stand anxiously on the cliff, their eyes fixed on the top of the rope bridge.

Indiana's head appears above the cliff, and slowly and painfully, he pulls himself upward toward safety. He grins at his friends,

Production still by
Keith Hamshere
Center: Cinematographer Douglas
Slocombe (left of camera) lines
up a shot on location in Sri
Lanka. Photo by
Keith Hamshere
Bottom: Production painting by
Elliot Scott

EXTERIOR: MAYAPORE VILLAGE

*A multitude of children have followed Indiana, Willie, and Short
Round; as they see the villagers ahead, they run past them
toward their homes.*

*Now we hear shouts of joy from the peasants. The children
returning home run to meet their parents, who are rushing out to
greet them.*

*There is laughter and tears as families are reunited. Indiana sees
the old shaman approaching with the chieftain and the village
elders.*

*The shaman touches his fingers to his forehead and bows. The
three travelers return his greeting, and the shaman is quite
moved as he speaks to Indiana.*

SHAMAN: We know you are coming back *(indicating the countryside)* when life returned to our village. Now you can see the
magic of the rock…you bring back.

*The old shaman smiles wisely at Indiana. Indy takes the stone
out of his bag and gives it to the shaman.*

INDIANA: Yes, I understand its power now.

*Willie watches the shaman take it reverently and bow to them.
The shaman joins the elders and they walk to the village's small
sacred mound. Indy and Willie stay back. They see him kneel
and replace the stone in its niche.*

WILLIE *(to Indiana):* You could've kept it.
INDIANA: Ah, what for? They'd just put it in a museum. It'd be
another rock collecting dust.
WILLIE: But then it would have given you your fortune and glory.

Indy shrugs and then smiles slyly.

INDIANA: Anything can happen. It's a long way to Delhi.

She looks at him like he's crazy.

WILLIE: No, thanks. No more adventures with you, Dr. Jones.
INDIANA: Sweetheart, after all the fun we've had together.
WILLIE: If you think I'm going to Delhi with you, or anyplace else after all the trouble you've gotten me into! Think again, buster! I'm goin' home to Missouri, where they never feed you snakes before ripping your heart out, and lowering you into hot pits! *This* is not my idea of a swell time.

She turns and walks toward the villagers.

WILLIE (continuing) (calling to a villager): Excuse me, sir? I need a guide to Delhi.

Suddenly the bullwhip CRACKS and wraps around her waist. Startled, Willie looks angry as Indiana reels her in, pulling her toward him and into his arms.

They start to kiss, and are suddenly drenched by a spray of water. They look up to see Short Round sitting on the baby elephant, and laughing at his joke.

SHORT ROUND: Very funny! Very funny!

Indiana and Willie laugh and return to their kiss as the villagers run up and crowd around them. Short Round covers his eyes.

SHORT ROUND: Uh, oh!

THE END

Production stills by
Keith Hamshere

CREDITS

PRODUCTION STAFF

Directed by . . . . STEVEN SPIELBERG
Produced by . . . . ROBERT WATTS
Story by . . . . GEORGE LUCAS
Screenplay by . . . . WILLARD HUYCK & GLORIA KATZ
Executive Producers . . . . GEORGE LUCAS, FRANK MARSHALL
Music by . . . . JOHN WILLIAMS
Editor . . . . MICHAEL KAHN, A.C.E.
Director of Photography . . . . DOUGLAS SLOCOMBE
Production Designer . . . . ELLIOT SCOTT
Costume Designer . . . . ANTHONY POWELL
Associate Producer . . . . KATHLEEN KENNEDY
Casting . . . . MIKE FENTON, C.S.A., JANE FEINBERG, C.S.A.,
MARY SELWAY BUCKLEY, MARCI LIROFF
Second Unit Director . . . . MICHAEL MOORE
Choreography by . . . . DANNY DANIELS

CAST

Indiana Jones . . . . HARRISON FORD
Willie Scott . . . . KATE CAPSHAW
Short Round . . . . KE HUY QUAN
Mola Ram . . . . AMRISH PURI
Chattar Lal . . . . ROSHAN SETH
Captain Blumburtt . . . . PHILIP STONE
Lao Che . . . . ROY CHIAO

SUPPORTING CAST

Wu Han . . . . DAVID YIP
Kao Kan . . . . RIC YOUNG
Chen . . . . CHUA KAH JOO
Maitre d' . . . . REX NGUI
Chief Henchman . . . . PHILIP TANN
Weber . . . . DAN AYKROYD
Chinese Pilot . . . . AKIO MITAMURA
Chinese Co-Pilot . . . . MICHAEL YAMA
Shaman . . . . D. R. NANAYAKKARA
Chieftain . . . . DHARMADASA KURUPPU

Sajnu	STANY DE SILVA
Village Women	RUBY DE MIEL, D.M. DENAWAKE, I. SERASINGHE
Village Child	DHARSHANA PANANGALA
Little Maharajah	RAJ SINGH
Merchant #1	FRANK OLEGARIO
Merchant #2	AHMED EL-SHENAWI
Eel Eater	ART REPOLA
Sacrifice Victim	NIZWAR KARANJ
Chief Guard	PAT ROACH
Guard	MOTI MAKAN
Temple Guards	MELLAN MITCHELL, BHASKER PATEL
1st Boy in Cell	ARJUN PANDHER
2nd boy in Cell	ZIA GELANI

TECHNICAL CREDITS

UNITED KINGDOM PRODUCTION CREW

Assistant Director	DAVID TOMBLIN
Production Supervisor	JOHN DAVIS
Production Manager	PATRICIA CARR
Second Assistant Directors	ROY BUTTON, STEVE HARDING

UNITED STATES PRODUCTION CREW

Production Manager	ROBERT LATHAM BROWN
First Assistant Director	LOUIS RACE
Second Assistant Director	LOUIS G. FRIEDMAN
Sound Design	BEN BURTT
Visual Effects Supervisor	DENNIS MUREN
Mechanical Effects Supervisor	GEORGE GIBBS
Stunt Arranger (Studio)	VIC ARMSTRONG
Stunt Arranger (Location)	GLENN RANDALL
Production Controller	ARTHUR CARROLL
Marketing and Promotion	SIDNEY GANIS
Script Supervisors	PHYLLIS TOWNSHEND, PAMELA MANN FRANCIS
Production Secretary	LINDA RABIN
Additional Photography	PAUL BEESON, B.S.C.
Operating Cameramen	CHIC WATERSON, DAVID WORLEY
Assistant Cameramen	ROBIN VIDGEON, CHRIS TANNER
Second Assistant Cameramen	TONY BROWN, DANNY SHELMERDINE
Dolly Grips	COLIN MANNING, JOHN FLEMMING
Camera Maintenance	NOBBY GODDEN
Sound Mixer	SIMON KAYE
Boom Operator	DAVID SUTTON
Sound Maintenance	TAFFY HAINES
Chief Art Director	ALAN CASSIE
Art Director	ROGER CAIN
Set Decorator	PETER HOWITT
Assistant Art Directors	PETER RUSSELL, STEPHEN SCOTT
Production Illustrators	EDWARD VERREAUX, ANDREW G. PROBERT
Draughtsman	RICHARD HOLLAND

Construction Manager	BILL WELCH
Property Master	BARRY WILKINSON
Scenic Artist	TED MICHELL
Production Buyer	JOHN LANZER
Chief Modeller	DEREK HOWARTH
Modellers	KEITH SHORT, BRIAN MUIR, VALERIE CHARLTON, STUART SMITH
Chief SFX. Technician	RICHARD CONWAY
Floor Effects Supervisor	DAVID WATKINS
Senior SFX. Technicians	TREVOR NEIGHBOUR, DAVID WATSON
SFX. Technicians	BOB HOLLOW, BRIAN MORRISON, RODGER SHAW
SFX. Assistants	PETER DAVEY, STEPHEN HAMILTON, JOSS WILLIAMS
Chief SFX. Wireman	BOB WIESINGER
Wardrobe Supervisor	RON BECK
Assistant Costume Designer	JOANNA JOHNSTON
Wardrobe Mistress	JANET TEBROOKE
Wardrobe Master	PATRICK WHEATLEY
Makeup Supervisor	TOM SMITH
Chief Makeup Artist	PETER ROBB-KING
Makeup Artists	LINDA DE VETTA, DICKIE MILLS, JOHN WEBBER
Chief Hairdresser	COLIN JAMISON
Hairdresser	JANET JAMISON
Unit Publicist	SUSAN D'ARCY
Stillsman	KEITH HAMSHERE

POST-PRODUCTION SERVICES
PROVIDED BY SPROCKET SYSTEMS
A DIVISION OF LUCASFILM LTD.

Re-recording Mixers	BEN BURTT, GARY SUMMERS, RANDY THOM
Assistant Film Editors	COLIN WILSON, BRUCE GREEN, STEVE KEMPER
Supervising Dialogue Editor	LAUREL LADEVICH
Dialogue Editors	GLORIA S. BORDERS, RICHARD HYMNS

Sound Effects Editors	JOHN BENSON, TERESA ECKTON, KEN FISCHER, SUZANNE FOX
Assistant Sound Editors	TOM CHRISTOPHER, KATHLEEN KORTH, MARY HELEN LEASMAN, JOHN WATSON, CHRISTOPHER WEIR
Sound Assistants	KAREN HARDING, STEVE KLOCKSIEM
Foley Artist	DENNIE THORPE
Audio Engineers	HOWARD W. HAMMERMAN, TOMLINSON HOLMAN, BRIAN KELLY
Audio Technicians	TOM JOHNSON, TOM MARTIN, GARY RYDSTROM, DAWN WARNEKING, KRIS HANDWERK WISKES
Sprocket Systems Administration	JAMES KESSLER, CATHERINE COOMBS, K.C. HODENFIELD, SUSAN LEAHY
Supervising Music Editor	KENNETH WANNBERG
Music Recording Mixer	LYLE BURBRIDGE
Orchestrations	HERB SPENCER
Music Recording Consultant	BRUCE BOTNICK
Dance Sequence Playback Arranged by	PETER HOWARD
Assistant Choreographer	CAROLINE HAMILTON
Production Accountant	GEORGE MARSHALL
Location Accountant	STEFANO PRIORI
Assistant Production Accountant	TONY MILLER
Assistant to Production Controller	BARBARA HARLEY
Research	DEBORAH FINE
Indian Advisor	CRISTI JANAKI RATHOD
Assistant to Mr. Lucas	JANE BAY
Assistant to Mr. Marshall	MARY T. RADFORD
Assistant to Ms. Kennedy	KATE BARKER
Secretaries to Mr. Spielberg	KATHLEEN SWITZER, PATSY DE LORD
Secretary to Mr. Watts	REBECCA WEST
Studio Teachers	ADRIA LATER, JANET WILLIS
Transport Manager	VIC MINAY
Animal Handler	MIKE CULLING
Mr. Ford's Stand-in	JACK DEARLOVE
Marketing Coordinator	SUSAN TREMBLY
Chargehand Standby Props	JOE DIPPLE, BERNIE HEARN
Chargehand Dressing Props	CHARLES IXER, PETER WALLIS
Prop Storeman	TOMMY BACON
Standby Prop	MARTIN KINGSLEY
Assistant Construction Manager	BERT LONG
Construction Storeman	DAVE MIDDLETON
Master Carpenter	ANTHONY YOUD
Master Plasterer	KENNETH CLARKE
Supervising Chargehand Plasterer	KENNETH BARLEY
Master Painter	BILL BEECHAM
Supervising Rigger	RED LAWRENCE
Supervising Stagehand	MICKY DRISCOLL
Standby Carpenter	STEPHEN HARGREAVES
Standby Plasterer	RAY STAPLES
Standby Painter	BOB BETTS
Standby Rigger	FRED CRAWFORD
Standby Stagehand	GEORGE GIBBONS
Gaffer	MARTIN EVANS
Best Boy	RAY MEEHAN
Rigging Gaffer	TOMMY BROWN
Drapes	BARRY WILSON

SECOND UNIT (LONDON)

Second Unit Director	FRANK MARSHALL
First Assistant Directors	DAVID BRACKNELL, MICHAEL HOOK
Operating Cameraman	WALLY BYATT
Assistant Cameraman	KEITH BLAKE
Second Assistant Cameraman	MARTIN KENZIE
Dolly Grip	JIM KANE
Floor Effects Supervisor	DAVID HARRIS
Gaffer	EAMONN DUNNE
Chief Makeup Artist	CONNIE REEVE
Hairdresser	HILARY HAINES
Standby Props	STEVE SHORT, SIMON WILKINSON
Standby Carpenter	ROGER DAWSON
Standby Plasterer	MICHAEL QUINN
Standby Painter	TONY CACCAVALE
Standby Rigger	TOM PARKER
Standby Stagehand	GEORGE KING

CALIFORNIA

Second Unit Director	GLENN RANDALL
Director of Photography	ALLEN DAVIAU
Art Director	JOE JOHNSTON
Location Manager	RICHARD VANE
Production Co-Ordinator	LATA RYAN
Operating Cameramen	JOHN CONNOR, JOHN STEVENS
First Assistant Cameraman	ERIC ENGLER
Key Grip	KEN PHELPS
Gaffer	PAT KIRKWOOD
Property Master	DANNY COLANGELO
Wardrobe Mistress	BARBARA KASSEL
Makeup Artist	YVONNE CURRY
Hairdresser	LYNDA GURASICH
Stunt Co-Ordinator	DEAN RAPHAEL FERRANDINI
SFX. Supervisor	KEVIN PIKE
Raft Camera Mounts	ART VITARELLI
Transportation Co-Ordinator	DAVE MARDER
Sound Mixer	DAVID McMILLAN
Sound Boom Operator	STEPHEN POWELL
Stills Photographer	RALPH NELSON, JR.
Production Accountants	BONNE RADFORD, DIANE DANKWARDT
Ski Unit Co-Ordinator	CLIFFORD MANN
Producer's Secretary	ANNIE BERARDINI
Producer's Assistant	PATRICK CRANE

ASIAN UNIT (MACAU & SRI LANKA)

Assistant Director	CARLOS GIL
Second Assistant Director	IAN BRYCE
Script Supervisor	CERI EVANS

MACAU

Production Supervisor	VINCENT WINTER
Production Manager	PAY LING WANG
Assistant Director	PATTY CHAN
Location Manager	MAY LEUNG
Stills Photographer	JEFF MARKS

FACILITIES IN MACAU SUPPLIED BY
SALON FILMS (H.K.) LTD.

SRI LANKA

Production Supervisor	CHANDRAN RUTNAM
Location Manager	PETER BENNETT
Production Manager	WILLIE DE SILVA
Unit Manager	ASOKA PERERA
Assistant Director	RANJIT H. PEIRIS
Steadicam® Photography	GARRETT BROWN
Art Director	ERROL KELLY
Production Secretary	RITA DE SILVA
Sound Mixer	COLIN CHARLES
Boom Operator	GARY WEIR
Sound Maintenance	COLIN DANDRIDGE

FACILITIES IN SRI LANKA SUPPLIED BY
SRI LANKA LOCATION SERVICES LTD.

AERIAL UNIT

Second Unit Director	KEVIN DONNELLY
Director of Photography	JACK COOPERMAN, A.S.C.
Pilots	ART SCHOLL, LENNARD VON CLEMM, ROSS REYNOLDS
Jump Master	LARRY LEE PERKINS

VISUAL EFFECTS PRODUCED AT
INDUSTRIAL LIGHT & MAGIC

MARIN COUNTY

Chief Visual Effects Cameraman	MIKE McALISTER
Optical Photography Supervisor	BRUCE NICHOLSON
General Manager, ILM	TOM SMITH
Production Supervisor	WARREN FRANKLIN
Matte Painting Supervisor	MICHAEL PANGRAZIO
Modelshop Supervisor	LORNE PETERSON
Stop Motion Animation	TOM ST. AMAND
Supervising Stage Technician	PATRICK FITZSIMMONS
Animation Supervisor	CHARLES MULLEN
Supervising Visual Effects Editor	HOWARD STEIN
Visual Effects Cameraman	MIKE OWENS
Assistant Cameramen	KIM MARKS, PAT SWEENEY, RANDY JOHNSON, JOE FULMER
Production Coordinator	ARTHUR REPOLA
Stage Coordinator	EDWARD HIRSH
Optical Camera Operators	JOHN ELLIS, DAVID BERRY, DONALD CLARK
Optical Line-Up	TOM ROSSETER, ED JONES, PEG HUNTER
Lab Technicians	TIM GEIDEMAN, JEFF DORAN, LOUIS RIVERA
Effects Creative Consultant	PHIL TIPPETT
Stop Motion Technicians	DAVID SOSALLA, RANDY OTTENBERG, SEAN CASEY
Matte Artists	CHRISTOPHER EVANS, FRANK ORDAZ, CAROLEEN GREEN
Matte Camera Supervisor	CRAIG BARRON
Matte Photography	DAVID FINCHER, DEBORAH MORGAN
Storyboard Artists	STAN FLEMING, PHIL NORWOOD

Chief Model Makers	PAUL HUSTON, BARBARA GALLUCCI, CHARLIE BAILEY, EASE OWYEUNG, MICHAEL FULMER
Model Makers	WESLEY SEEDS, BARBARA AFFONSO LARRY TAN, MARC THORPE, SCOTT MARSHALL, CHUCK WILEY, PETE RONZANI, JEFF MANN, IRA KEELER, RICHARD DAVIS, WILLIAM GEORGE, MIKE COCHRANE
Head Effects Animator	BRUCE WALTERS
Effects Animators	BARBARA BRENNAN, JACK MONGOVAN, ELLEN LICHTWARDT, REBECCA PETRULLI, SEAN TURNER, SUKI STERN
Visual Effects Editor	MICHAEL GLEASON
Assistant Effects Editor	MICHAEL MOORE
Additional Photography	RICK FICHTER
Stage Technicians	BOB FINLEY III, DICK DOVA, JOHN McLEOD, DAVE CHILDERS, HAROLD COLE, LANCE BRACKETT, MERLIN OHM, MIKE SPEAKMAN
Miniature Pyrotechnics	TED MOEHNKE, PETER STOLZ, BOB FINLEY, JR.
Still Photography	TERRY CHOSTNER, KERRY NORDQUIST, ROBERTO McGRATH
Engineering	MICHAEL MacKENZIE, WADE CHILDRESS, GREG BEAUMONTE, JERRY JEFFRESS, KRIS BROWN
Machine Shop	UDO PAMPEL, CHRISTOPHER RAND
Location Coordinator	PATTY BLAU
Administrative Staff	CHRISSIE ENGLAND, CHERYL DURHAM, SUSAN MONAHAN, PAULA KARSH, KATHY SHINE, KAREN AYERS, KAREN DUBE, NED GORMAN, GEOFFREY de VALOIS
Effects Processing	MONACO LABS
Negative Cutters	JACK HOOPER, TOM HOOPER, GARY BURRITT
Color Timers	JIM SCHURMANN, TERRY CLABORN
Titles and Additional Optical Effects	MODERN FILM EFFECTS
Additional Optical Line-Up	JACQUES PROTAY

STUNTS

VIC ARMSTRONG	WENDY LEECH
FELIX SILLA	ROY ALON
DICKIE BEER	PETER BRACE
ANDREW BRADFORD	TERRY CADE
GRAEME CROWTHER	DEAN RAPHAEL FERRANDINI
TERRY FORRESTAL	MARIETTA GILLMAN
TED GROSSMAN	REG HARDING
FRANK HENDSON	NICK HOBBS
BILLY HORRIGAN	DONNA KEEGAN
BRONCO McLAUGHLIN	WAYNE MICHAELS
GARETH MILNE	GREG POWELL
GLENN RANDALL	BILL REED
DOUG ROBINSON	DENISE RYAN
COLIN SKEAPING	ROCKY TAYLOR
TIP TIPPING	MALCOLM WEAVER
CHRIS WEBB	JASON WHITE
CHUCK WATERS	FRED WASHBURN

DANCERS

DEBBIE ASTELL	MAUREEN BACCHUS
CORINNE BARTON	CAROL BEBBINGTON
SHARON BOONE	ELIZABETH BURVILLE
MARISA CAMPBELL	CHRISTINE CARTWRIGHT
ANDREA CHANCE	JAN COLTON
LOUISE DALGLEISH	LORRAINE DOYLE
VANESSA FIELDWRIGHT	BRENDA GLASSMAN
ELAINE GOUGH	SUE HADLEIGH
SARAH-JANE HASSELL	SAMANTHA HUGHES
JULIE KIRK	DEIRDRE LAIRD
VICKI McDONALD	NINA McMAHON
JULIA MARSTAND	GAYNOR MARTINE
LISA MULIDORE	DAWN REDDALL
REBEKKAH SEKYI	CLARE SMALLEY
LEE SPRINTALL	JENNY TURNOCK
RUTH WELBY	

"ANYTHING GOES"
MUSIC & LYRICS BY COLE PORTER

THANKS TO THE GOVERNMENTS OF SRI LANKA
AND MACAU FOR THEIR HELP

PHOTOGRAPHED AT THORN EMI-ELSTREE STUDIOS, BOREHAMWOOD, ENGLAND AND ON LOCATION IN SRI LANKA, MACAU, MAMMOTH MOUNTAIN AND THE TUOLOMNE AND AMERICAN RIVERS IN CALIFORNIA

THANKS TO: BALFOUR BEATTY NUTTAL VICTORIA PROJECT, SRI LANKA · PHYSICAL CONDITIONING FOR MR. FORD BY BODY BY JAKE, INC. · LIGHTING EQUIPMENT AND CREW FROM LEE ELECTRIC LTD. · METALWORK BY NORANK ENGINEERING LTD. · RAFTS BY MARAVIA CORPORATION · CATERING BY LOCATION CATERERS · AUBURN DUESENBERG CONSTRUCTED BY SPECIALTY CARS · PRODUCTION VEHICLES COURTESY OF GMC TRUCK AND BUS · AIR TRANSPORTATION BY PAN AM AND AIR LANKA · ADR BY MAYFLOWER RECORDING LTD. AND WARNER HOLLYWOOD STUDIOS · MUSIC RECORDING AT METRO-GOLDWYN-MAYER

THANKS TO REED SMOOT
COLOR BY RANK LABORATORIES®
PRINTS BY DELUXE®
LENSES AND PANAFLEX® CAMERAS BY PANAVISION®
A LUCASFILM LTD. PRODUCTION
ORIGINAL SOUNDTRACK ON POLYDOR RECORDS AND TAPES
NOVELIZATION FROM BALLANTINE BOOKS